THE BOOK OF
CREECH ST MICHAEL

THE BOOK OF
CREECH ST MICHAEL

THE PARISH AND ITS PEOPLE
JUNE SMALL

First published in Great Britain in 2000

British Library Cataloguing-in-Publication Data
A CIP record for this title is available from the British Library

ISBN 1 84114 093 4

HALSGROVE
PUBLISHING, MEDIA AND DISTRIBUTION

Halsgrove House
Lower Moor Way
Tiverton, Devon EX16 6SS
Tel: 01884 243242
Fax: 01884 243325
email: sales@halsgrove.com
website: http://www.halsgrove.com

Printed and bound in Great Britain by Bookcraft Ltd., Midsomer Norton.

Foreword

This project was started many years ago and was prompted by an interest in the results of the school study of the parish of Creech St Michael in 1970. In 1973 the school celebrated its 100th anniversary, an exhibition was mounted in the church and, together with the children, I worked on the history once again. For several years I attended a study class at the Somerset Record Office and found a wealth of information about the parish which I wanted to share with others.

I was kept busy for several years with our business as well as promoting British farming; and then 2000 arrived and I decided that my research had to be completed in this year. As I had only been looking at records for my own interest in the beginning, I had not recorded sources, but the majority of the information came from the Somerset Record Office, the Rural Life Museum in Glastonbury, the Local History Library in Taunton and from talking to people in the area. Many interesting articles were found in local newspapers of the time and I was easily sidetracked by items unrelated to my subject.

Having lived in the parish for 40 years and attended a wedding and a funeral of a true parishioner (a local sign of acceptance as a newcomer), I am now part of the history and very happy to share my research, thereby hopefully stimulating an interest in gathering more information for the future. The changes over the last 1000 years have shaped the parish as we see it in 2000, and all those past inhabitants who have contributed in making the landscape as we recognise it today should be remembered and recorded.

JUNE SMALL
CREECH ST MICHAEL, 2000

The Way family outside their house at the beginning of Charlton Road.
On the backside of the house facing up the road Joe Way had a grocery shop.

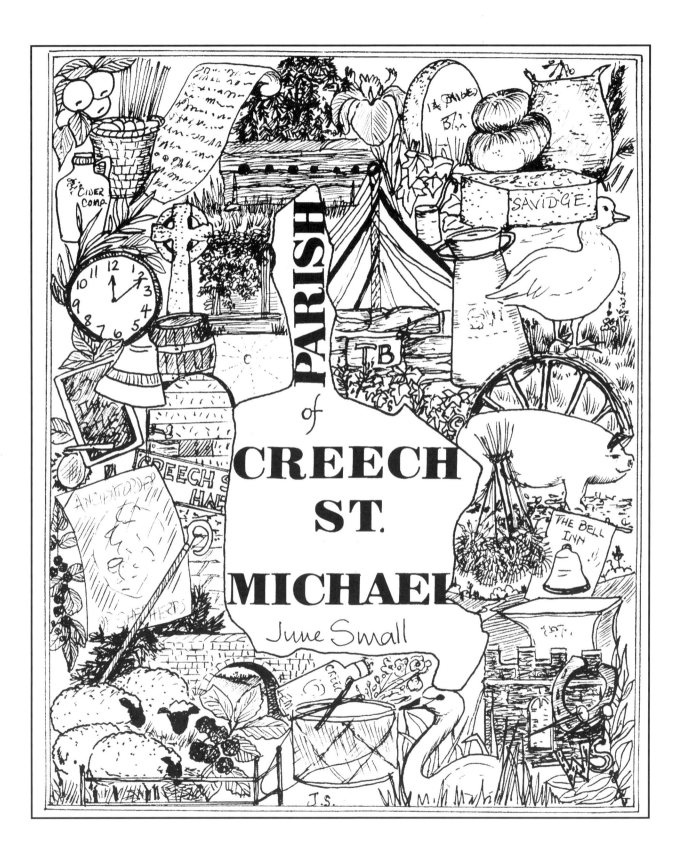

ACKNOWLEDGEMENTS

Thank you to all who may have contributed in any way, however small, to this book and to the patient staff at the Somerset Record Office who answered my often naïve questions. Thank you to all who kindly lent photos, named people in them and told me wonderful stories. Many people loaned precious family photographs for this book and I am particularly grateful to: Margaret Adams, Margaret Bartlett, Fred and Mariene Batstone, Jim Cole, Nora Drewe, June Fowler, Brian Foxwell, the Hopkins family, Phyl Powell, Les and Betty Richards, Ron Smith, Madge Stace, Mr and Mrs Stocker, the Sweeting family, Mr and Mrs Thatcher, Jean Walters and Ron Welch. Special thanks to my husband, Robin, who listened to every snippet of interest and never looked bored. Lastly to my friend Gill Norris who on hearing that I was a novice computer user and was experiencing difficulties came to my rescue. My grateful thanks for her painstaking efforts.

The Miss Blackmores, Lizzie and Cassie.

Meet at the Bell Inn, 1940s.

A. and C. Bishop's butcher's van. D. Hooper was the assistant.

CONTENTS

In 1559 Creechwood comprised some 50 acres of mainly oak and ash but in 1619 the timber was felled from the wood and the purchaser told to make good the ground after removal.

The Bridgwater-Taunton canal brought many industries to the parish. Here at the bridge on the main village road there was once a brewery and a coalyard as well as a lemonade maker!

Chapter 1
In The Beginning

There is much debate amongst historians as to the origin of the name Creech St Michael. 'Cruch' is Welsh for hill, although the slight incline on which the church stands can hardly be termed a 'hill'. St Michael is the patron saint of churches on hills, but is also said to be the patron saint of Celts. As in early records Creech is also called Michael Creek, it is more likely that it refers to the position it held at a small creek on the Tone where boats would come in. It is referred to in the churchwardens' accounts also as a stopping point for travellers to and from Bridgwater and further west. At times the name appears variously as Crice, Cruk, Criche and Mitchell Creek. The *Victorian History of Somerset* refers to Muchel Creech, meaning great, and Little Creech, where the animal centre is, as being part of the parish until 1884 when it was transferred to West Hatch parish.

An early charter in 854 shows a grant made by Aethlwulf, King of Wessex, to Eathstan, Bishop of Winchester, in which 'that parte of Creech west of a stream which runs through Northend to the River Tone' was included. In 882, St Neot, a friend of Alfred the Great, is recorded as having visited Creech. William I gave Criche to Robert of Mortaine (William's step-brother), whose son then gave it to Montacute:

William of Mortaine grants to the Cluniac Monks for the good of his soul and the souls of his father, Robert, and his mother, Matilda, the Church of St Peter near his castle of Montacute and gives the Borough and its market and tolls, castle, chapel with orchards and vineyards.

Also included was the manor of Crice with Hamme.

In 1269, Henry III granted and confirmed 'a market to be held in the same place Tuesday in the Manor of Crice in the County of Somerset', also:

... a fair at the same place every year, lasting three days, namely on the eve, day and morrow of St Augustine's Day in May, unless that market and fair be to the detriment of neighbouring markets and fairs.

DOMESDAY 1086

When William the Conqueror came to the English throne, he felt it necessary to investigate the land he owned, the dues entitled to him and how the land was farmed. He sent his men out into the countryside to survey the land and, according to Anglo-Saxon Chronicles:

The King caused them to write down how much each man that was settled on the land in England held in land and cattle and how much it was worth.

From this came the Domesday Book, so called after the Day of Judgement from which there is no escape. It was to be one of the most important documents in English history. The entry for Creech reads as follows:

The King holds Crice, Gunhilde held it tempore regis Edward and paid

LAY SUBSIDY ROLLS

IN 1327 A LIST OF PEOPLE WHO WERE LIABLE TO PAY TAX WAS MADE FOR THE MANOR OF CREECH

De Rogero de Wellsford
Gilberto de Conertone
Stephano atte Breche
Waltero Molle
Stephano Noreys
Thoma Bonetheford
Juliana Tottheis
Johanna Hokers
Nicolao Redyene
Margaretta in the Lane
Willelmo Wiard
Heurico Pachet
Roberto Stonhard
Hugone Amains
Johanne Aude
Petro Preest
Petro Lontyng
Nicholato Exte
Julianna Cranston
Stephano Loneshaft
Waltero Talman
Petro Fleke
Alicia de Hamme
Amiana Forde
Richardo de Hamme
Willelmo Wheler
Nicolao Peny
Johanne Muleward
Willelmo Cabbal
Willelmo Pleystrete
Johanne Uphulle
Gilberto Walford
Odone de Langire

Willelmo Pile
Simone Webb
Thoma Long
De Johanne Smyt
Waltero Ande
Matilda atte Hurne
Roberto atte Pile
Roberto Mode
Willelmo de Hideberghe
Johanne Webbe
Roberto Driw
Willelmo Best
Willelmo Ayln
Wallero Hexte
Willelmo Berenger
Willelmo Herebyne
Richardo Mark
Johanne de Barton
Rogero Auger
Roberto atte Oke
Agnette Cherletone
De Florencin Carpenter
Godefrido de Edfield
Galfrodo de Mayns
Sbtax Thos Elys
Sbtax Willelmo Trivet

Summa totallis xxdicti
mannerii de Crych

FROM SUCH AN APPARENTLY SIMPLE LIST OF NAMES,
WE CAN LEARN A LOT ABOUT THE EARLY INHABITANTS OF CREECH. SOME NAMES NEED
TO BE SPOKEN OUT LOUD TO REVEAL THEIR MEANING – CONERTONE, FOR EXAMPLE,
SUGGESTS SOMEONE WHO LIVED ON A CORNER NEAR THE TONE,
AND CHERELETONE PERHAPS A WOMAN FROM CHARLTON.

OTHER NAMES REVEAL AN OCCUPATION SUCH AS WEBBE – A SPINNER, MULEWARD – A
MILLER, FLEKE – A BOWMAKER, AND FLORENCIN – A CARPENTER. PREEST MEANS PRIEST
AND WALFORD AND HAMME ARE BOTH PLACES OUTSIDE THE PARISH.
SOME SUCH NAMES CAN STILL BE FOUND TODAY
LIKE DRIWE AND SMYT.

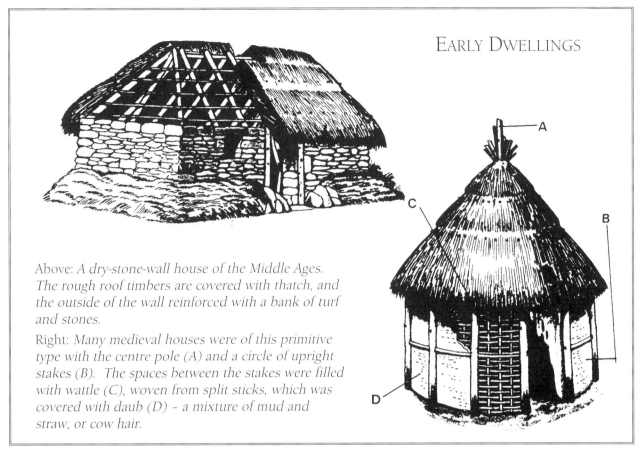

EARLY DWELLINGS

Above: *A dry-stone-wall house of the Middle Ages. The rough roof timbers are covered with thatch, and the outside of the wall reinforced with a bank of turf and stones.*

Right: *Many medieval houses were of this primitive type with the centre pole (A) and a circle of upright stakes (B). The spaces between the stakes were filled with wattle (C), woven from split sticks, which was covered with daub (D) – a mixture of mud and straw, or cow hair.*

geld for 10 hides. There is land for 8 ploughs, of this there are in demesne 6 hides where there are 2 ploughs and 6 serfs, 20 villeins and 10 bordars, with 6 ploughs and 4 hides, 1 riding horse, 10 beasts, 10 swine and 48 sheep. There is a mill paying 8 pence and 8 acres of meadow pasture and wood 1 league long and as much broad, it pays 9 pounds 4 shillings of white silver and when William de Moine received it as much. There is a fishery there but it does not belong to the ferme.

The King's officials did not write down everything they saw, for their job was to record land and its worth, so houses and churches were seldom mentioned, and only heads of families listed, so we do not have a true record of the entire population or of the buildings. We do know, however, that '20 villeins lived in Crice'. They were responsible for the manorial economy and their duties varied from place to place. They would plough, shear, carry goods and be

C14th Cider Press

responsible for guard duty. They would hold about 30 acres and 3 oxen on average, whilst bordars would hold about 5 acres and many owned oxen too. They would work on the lord's land and usually dwelt on the edge of the village (in some areas they were called cottars).

The serfs, of which there were six in Crice, were counted more as things than people and they did many of the menial jobs. They would help with the ploughing and harvesting and were allowed little free time.

The beasts were mainly oxen but there were also sheep and swine. The swine needed woods to forage in and such land was situated below Creechwood Terrace. Just a few trees now remain of the original wood. Pasture was probably larger than recorded, because when the moors flooded and remained under water for some time they were not counted in the survey as local people would have been foolish to say how lush the grass was when the moors were drained in summer.

The population would have been about four or five times the actual recorded number so it was in fact quite a large manor, and its position, by an important waterway crossing, significant.

WILLELM:

Husk Farm at the end of Laburnum Terrace.
Traces of a very old dwelling can be seen in the barns adjoining

Bridge over the rhines at Northend.

Chapter 2
Court Leets and The Vestry

These courts were held by the lord of the manor, usually in the manor house (which was Court Barton) to discuss parish affairs, changes of tenancy, regulation of the open-field system and infringements of property rights. These were the main issues but periodically the appointment of constables, jurymen and other parish duties took place. From the following examples from Court Leet records it will be seen how the clearing of water courses and the repair of bridges featured regularly in the proceedings. In the mid 1800s the church Vestry took over the duties of the Manor Courts and a very long tradition came to an end. In pre-Norman times, land in England was held by the lords who were given the rights by the king. The common people, who lived in the area, were beholden to the lord of the manor for their living. Some commoners had land and could work it but they were in the service of the lord of the manor. He had many rights in the parish such as grazing, timber, produce and work on the land from the peasants.

1756
We present a former presentment. William Tovyn to take up his sluice and cleanse his ditch leading from Lashpool Green (Charlton) to the River Tone as far as his land extendeth.

1758
We present the bridges over the rhines at North End to be repaired by this day fortnight.

David and Robert Bobbet to pay a fine amerced for their erecting a wall on the Lords waste according to a former presentment. Whereas several persons from this Manor plowing up and carrying away large quantities of earth from the common ground. Fined 2 shillings per load if detected.

1763
We present John Cooper for not keeping his bay to keep water in its proper course in George Thornes 14 acres. Ditch to be put into repair in 10 days or else we amerce him 10 shillings.

1766
We present Samuel Richards for building a barn at Langaller Heathfield being the Lords waste and for encroachment thereof.

We present John Franklin for an eves dropper.

1771
We present all persons that shall keep geese to have no right to the commons and waste ground of the Manor, except those who have a right to the said commons with horses, bullocks and sheep.

1779
The tenants of this Manor have a right to have used, time out of mind to draw the two sluices of shute water next adjoining, Ham Moor at all times upon floods or when the river is likely to overflow the grounds adjoining and in default of their refusing to renew the said barricade or to keeping the said bridge in good repair we amerce them 10 pounds.

1786
We amerce the Lord of the Manor for not repairing the pound walls.

1800
We amerce Bagot and Co for landing timber on the wastelands called Shippon Moor and destroying the common rights 3 pounds 3 shillings.

We amerce Robert Stodgell for opening a dangerous drain at Edgeboro (Adsborough) Hill and making an encroachment of the same.

1804
Robert Stodgell for digging stones and selling the same and destroying the common rights on wasteland at Creech Heathfield.

1806
Richard Manning for cutting and carrying away thistles from Sheepham Moor and destroying the common right.

1807
Johnathan Warre for hauling away turf at Charlton Marsh.

1808
Mr Stone (and 8 others) for lodging coal on Creech Common.

1814
The pound door being out of repair that the same ought to be repaired at the expense of the Lord of the Manor.

1853
Ham to Creech bridge was in a dilapidated and dangerous state. Farmer Bull of Knapp was responsible [10 years later it was still in need of repair].

1857
At the Court Leet the haywarden in charge of the village pound was directed to 'in no instance charge more fees for impounding stock than is directed and allowed by the Highways Act'.

VESTRY MEETINGS

The first Vestry meeting came about in the 1500s when the Court Leets were beginning to weaken and there was a need to create a new form of parish government to attend to the ever-increasing and broad spectrum of parish matters.

With the new Act relating to highways in the reign of Mary Tudor, the Vestry became responsible for appointing haywardens and for levying rates. They also had the churchwardens, constables, haywardens (responsible for impounding stray animals) and the overseers to manage, which meant they administered the care of the poor in the parish too.

Each Easter, appointments were made for the various jobs which were unpaid but statutory, and fines could be imposed on those refusing or failing to carry out their duty. Access to a rota system meant that everyone took their turn at reasonable intervals. Overall responsibility by common law was in the hands of the vicar.

In 1833 the overseers were instructed:

On any person coming to inhabit your parish and become chargeable there not having a lawful settlement there not bringing with them a certificate of their being settled elsewhere nor giving security for the discharge of your parish, you are to make complaint thereof to the same two Justices of Peace of this division in order so the examination and removal of such a person in the place of his or

her last settlement. An unmarried mother being pregnant is deemed chargeable and may be removed.

A typical notice which would have been pinned to the church door for all to see reads as follows:

Notice is hereby given that a Vestry meeting will be held at the Parish Church on Friday next at 11 o'clock in the forenoon for the purpose of inspecting and settling the churchwardens' accounts and other parish business Noted this day of June 1824.

In the same year the following was reported:

Lawrence Gudridge is paying on Wednesday next into the hands of the overseers the sum of £20 for the maintenance and support of a female bastard child that Elizabeth Sealey was delivered of May 4th last and of which he is the reputed father that the sum be accepted in full compensation and the said Lawrence Gudridge released of full support of the child.

Parish officers often found deputies when it was their year of office. Women, according to their estate, were included in the office holding but they usually found a man to deputise (in return for payment of course). In 1825 the Vestry:

... determined to allow 5shs a week toward the maintenance of Mary Dyer, wife of William Dyer, late of Creech Mills, and it was also agreed that her brother, Mr John Dyer, shall forthwith look out for a residence for her, but not too near the mill and should she continue in health that the said John Dyer agrees to take her to his own house and this after his wife's confinement.

[There was also a] meeting of the Vestry to consider the propriety of apprehending William Dyer for going away and leaving his wife chargeable to the parish. [The] Vestry agreed to give Mr Boon the sum of 4 pounds for apprehending and bringing the above named William Dyer to the parish officers of Creech.

Again we read of a 'Vestry meeting to consider trouble over the non-repairing of an alleged common and ancient prime way from the village to the village of Ham.'

At this time, 1825, crime was also clearly something of a problem:

Notice is hereby given that in consequence of the numerous and almost nightly depredations and robberies committed by a set of dissolute and lawless plunderers, it is determined that a Vestry shall be called for Friday next at 11 o'clock forenoon for the purpose of looking into the consequences... of the forming of a parish association for the mutual protection of the property and for the purpose of bringing if possible the offenders to justice. Signed Henry Cresswell Vicar.

N.B. It is hoped that the principle inhabitants of the parish will attend to further their device and assistance in the necessary objective.

Report was made that:

There are many aged and infirm persons in the parish of Creech at present in distressed circumstances due to the inclement weather and other causes. I hereby give notice of a Vestry meeting on Wednesday next at 11 o'clock of the forenoon for the purpose of enquiring into their wants and where necessary, to afford extra relief during the winter quarter. It is requested that the churchwardens and overseers of the poor attend and do their duty, and it is hoped that other respectable payers of the parish will also be ready to give advice and assistance where common humanity requires it.

The outcome of this meeting was given as follows:

At a Vestry held this day it was agreed to afford extra relief to the industrious poor during the severe weather, such relief not to extend any longer than 25th March. The memorandum of such relief is entered in Mr Wyborn's Parish Book.

Feeding the poor. 1300

Above: *The road at Ham leading to the mill, an important landing place for boats on the Tone. The small road to the left leads to the bridge which featured as 'in need of repair' throughout parish history.*

Right: *Ham Bridge over the River Tone.*

COUNTY OF SOMERSET, (TO WIT,) DIVISION OF TAUNTON.

WE, *whose Hands and Seals are hereunto set, being Two of the King's Justices, assigned to keep his Peace in the said County, and also to here and determine divers Felonies, Trespasses, and other Misdemeanors therein committed; do by these Presents Nominate and Appoint*

John Bucknell William Morris and Timothy Elias Wyborn —

being substantial Householders
of the Parish of Creech Saint Michael *in the said Division, to be Overseers of the Poor of the said Parish, for the Year ensuing, according to the Directions of the Statute in that Case made and provided. Given under our Hands and Seals, the* ninth *Day of* April *in the Year of our Lord, 183* 3

AND for your better and more effectually executing the said Office, we do hereby make known unto You as follows:

THAT YOU, together with the Churchwardens of your parish for the time being, under the Penalty of TWENTY SHILLINGS each, are to meet once in every Month in your Church, upon the Sunday in the Afternoon, to confer together, consider of, and take Order, (with the consent of two Justices of the division) for setting to work the Children of all such whose Parents shall not be thought able to maintain them; and also for providing Relief for such Poor Persons as are lame, old, blind, or unable to work: And that you enter into a Book, to be kept for that purpose, the Names of all such Persons receiving Relief, and the occasion that brought them under the necessity.

THAT no Vestry shall be holden untill at least three days' Public Notice shall have been given and of the Place and Hour of holding the same, and the special purpose thereof, by publishing such Notice in the Church or Chapel, on some Sunday during or immediately after Divine Service, and by affixing the same on the principal door of the Church or Chaple.

IF the Clergyman shall not be present at such Vestry, a Chairman is to be appointed from one of the Inhabitants, by votes, to preside at such Vestry; and that Minutes of the proceedings be entered in a Book, and signed by the Chairman, and any other of the Inhabitants present.

EVERY Inhabitant present Assessed by the last Rate at £50. per Annum to have One Vote, and One other Vote for every £25. at which he was so Rated over and above £50. per Annum, provided, no Person shall be entitled to more than Six Votes.

THAT no Person, who shall have refused or neglected to pay any Rate due from him, which shall have been demanded, shall be entitled to vote or be present at a Vestry, until he shall have paid the same.

THAT all Vestry Books, Rates, Accounts, &c. shall be kept by such Person, and in such place as a majority of the Vestry shall direct.

PENALTY for destroying, obliterating, or injuring such Books, &c. or refusing to deliver them up to the Person so appointed, or to deposit them as ordered by the Vestry, not exceeding £50. nor less than £2. as shall be adjudged by two Justices.

YOU and the Churchwardens, with the consent of your Parishioners or Inhabitants in Vestry, may purchase or hire a House or Houses in your Parish, and contract with such for lodgings, maintaining, and employing all such Poor of your Parish as shall desire Relief: and if any person shall refuse to be lodged in such House, he or she shall be put out of the Book, and not entitled to Relief, unless an order shall have been made by one Justice to relieve such Persons at their own homes; and with the consent of one Justice of the Peace, your Parish may join with any adjacent Parish in purchasing or hiring a House for the purpose aforesaid; and you may contract with the Churchwardens and Overseers of any other Parish, for lodging or maintaining of any of your Poor.

YOU and the Churchwardens, or the greater part of them, (by the consent of any two Justices of the Peace, in and for the said Division,) are to bind any such Children as aforesaid, being more than nine, and under the age of Fifteen Years, to be Apprentices where they shall see convenient. And the Persons to whom they are bound are obliged to receive and provide for them, and to execute one part of the Indenture, whereby they are bound, under the Penalty of Forfeiting TEN POUNDS.

ON any Person coming to inhabit in your Parish, and becoming chargeable thereto, not having a lawful Settlement there, nor bringing with them a Certificate of their being settled elsewhere, nor giving Security for the discharge of your Parish, You are to make complaint thereof to some two Justices of the Peace, of this Division, in order to the Examination and Removal of such Person to the place of his or her last legal Settlement.

AN unmarried woman being pregnant, is deemed chargeable, and may be removed.

THAT orders of removal will in no case be granted, (except in cases of Unmarried Women with Child, and other urgent occasions,) unless Seven Days' Notice of an intended application for an Order, shall have been given *by the Clerk of the Magistrates*, to the Overseers of the Parish, in which the *Pauper* is supposed to be settled.

THAT the said Clerk, or his assistant, will take in writing all examinations, in cases of settlement, and produce the same before the Justices (except upon urgent occasions) full Seven Days previous to their granting or refusing any Order or Removal, and that the Overseers of the Poor are required to produce the Pauper and other necessary Witnesses at the expiration of such Seven or more Days, (as may be convenient) to be examined by the Justices on oath.

THAT upon all applications for the Recovery of the Poor's Rate, the Justices will require the Rate Book to be produced, to shew the Rate to be legal, before a Summons will be granted.

TO all which ends and purposes, You are to raise weekly, or otherwise, by Taxation of every Inhabitant, Parson, Vicar, and other and of every Occupier of Lands, Houses, Tythes, &c. in your said Parish, which Rate and Assessment is to be allowed by two Justices of the Peace of this County. And you are to give, or cause to be given, public Notice in the Church, of every Rate or Assessment for the relief of the Poor, allowed by the Justices of the Peace, on the next Sunday after the same shall have been so allowed; no such Rate being valid or sufficient to collect or raise the same, unless such Notice shall have been given. And you are to permit every Payer thereto to inspect every such Rate at all seasonable Times.

THAT the Overseers of the Poor will not be confined in Office *upon their own request*, for any succeeding year, unless they shall have fully complied with the Law, relating to their accounts; and that all Penalties for neglect of duty, will be strictly inflicted.

THAT any Parish wishing to have a Select Vestry for the affairs of the Poor, in pursuance of the Act 59 Geo. III. cap. 12. must make application to the Justices at the Petty Sessions, who will thereupon appoint such Persons as shall have been elected by the Inhabitants, in Vestry assembled.

THAT in all Parishes where Select Vestries are established, the Overseers are required to submit themselves to their directions, in all matters relating to the relief of the Poor.

THAT the Magistrates will, at the request of any Parish, appoint an Assistant Overseer, with such Salary as shall be agreed on by such Parish in Vestry.

T. TROOD, PRINTER, TAUNTON.

Official document for the appointment of three overseers of the poor of Creech in 1833.

Chapter 3
Poor Laws, Militia and Charities

Before the Black Death came to England and claimed so many lives, the Feudal Society assumed that each parish would care for their poor, but no laws governed how this should be achieved. In 1348 the Black Death arrived and by 1368 one third of the population of England and Wales had succumbed. Because of an acute shortage of labour, land lay uncultivated, animals died and villages were abandoned. Those able-bodied labourers who were left could demand high wages for their services. This caused unrest among the rural population so Edward III's government passed a Statute of Labour which forbade employers to pay the higher wages demanded. Land-owners were desperate for workers and largely ignored the law. This caused vagrant landless people or runaways to sell themselves to the highest bidder, so in 1386 the Poor Law Act was passed which forebade a person to move from his parish without authority. This law remained in place for hundreds of years. The law also stated that those unable to look after themselves should receive help from the parish. By 1450 and for the next 150 years, wars against France left many returning soldiers penniless vagrants. The problem was exacerbated by the fact that land-owners were putting increasing numbers of sheep onto the land rather than growing grain which had required a higher input of manual labour. In turn, the villages became depopulated and families tramped the roads destitute and homeless.

Recognising the problem, the Tudors set about finding a solution by passing the 1495 Beggars and Vagabonds Act and giving permission for people to beg but only in certain areas. If the law was violated, the penalty would be a beating or three days in the stocks. This Act also advised parishes on how to raise money for the poor. It exhorted the rich to fund charities, to give regular payments towards the upkeep of the poor and to use church collections.

By 1552 churchwardens were experiencing difficulties collecting sufficient funds to fulfil commitments, so it was suggested that each parish appoint two collectors to help, and funding became compulsory. Those failing to comply found themselves in court. Elizabeth I made the Justices of the Peace responsible for superintending the work of the parish officers and churchwardens. In addition, several trusted householders, to be known as overseers of the poor, were elected yearly to raise funds from the parish '... by taxation of every inhabitant and every occupier of land in the said parish in such competent sums of money they shall think fit'.

At the end of the year, the overseers had to give detailed accounts to the Justices and it is those accounts which provide an insight into the life of the parish for many years. Unfortunately, in a desire to see as little rate paid as possible, many overseers acted mercilessly by turning people out of the parish, especially unmarried pregnant women, as the infant would be a burden on the parish. Paupers' children were forcibly apprenticed. The job was a difficult one for an overseer with a conscience as he had to balance compassion with accounts.

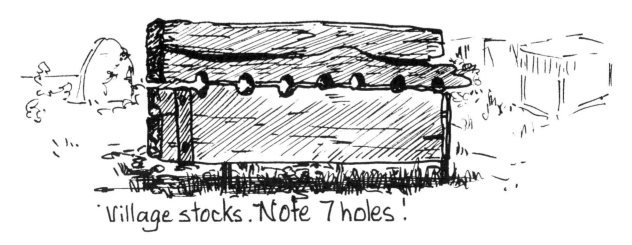

'Village stocks. Note 7 holes!'

THE FOLLOWING ARE NOTES FROM CREECH POOR BOOK:

1700s

Thomas Hearn - a pair of stockings	1s.3d.
Robt Slapp -a rug	6s.0d.
Mary Dyer - in want	1s.0d.
Coate for Chris Moores maide	2s.1d.
Robt Slapp - a pair of breeches	3s.6d.
Mary Hancock for keeping Will. Elsoms child 3 weeks	3s.6d.
Gave Thos Hearn for a loaf of bread	7d.
Moores child - a shifte and apron	3s.0d.
New pare of shoes for Millers boy	2s.4d.
Jo. Baron - a second hand coate	5s.0d.
Bed, bedstead, bolster, mattress and cord for Mary Fogarty	19s.0d.
New sheets, blanket, rug and two pillow cloths	18s.7d.
For labour of carrying them to Creech	1s.0d.
New shifte and petticoate for John Staces wife	6s.11d.
For glazing of Bryants house	8s.3½d.
Sack of coal for Mary Dyer	2s.2d.
Sarah Tarrs coffin and laying out	6s.0d.
Coffin, bell, grave and funeral expenses of Mary Way	14s.6d.
Mr Bryant for setting Will Bradfords shoulder	10s.6d.
Expenses for binding an apprentice	£1.0s.0d.
Paid for a new shovel for use in the parish	3s.8d.
Sam Bull coffin for Henry Baker	8s.0d.
Sam Bull for going after the coroner	10s.0d.
Sam Bull for digging the grave and attending burial	2s.0d.
To people to put him in his grave	1s.0d.
For liquor for the jury by order of the coroner	11s.6d.

1787

For taking out of pawn Sam Chappells coat	5s.9d.
Paid for expenses of going in procession round village	£3.16s.10d.
Paid for Culverwells axe which he had in pawn	6d.
Robert Kimberly for mending shoes of the poore	7s.7d.
20 sheaves of reed for Richard Kewers house	5s.0d.

1789

10 faggots of wood for Thos. White	1s.4d.
Bell and grave for Handoles child	3s.8d.
Robert Dinham pare of hogin gloves	1s.8d.
Mary Fry and Snook for going to Taunton, horse and Cart and turnpike	2s.9d.
Paid expenses for apprehending Geo. Cooking for Keeping him in custody 2 days and 1 night	12s.7½d.
Paid constables for their time	2s.6d.

CREECH POOR BOOK OF 1825 GIVES A LIST OF CRITERIA FOR QUALIFYING AS A PAUPER; OLD AND INFIRM, HAVING A SICK CHILD, OUT OF WORK, HAVING FIVE CHILDREN, WIDOW WITH CHILD, BASEBORN CHILD.

THE FOLLOWING EXTRACTS COME FROM TAUNTON COURTS OF JUSTICE RECORDS

1652
Upon the consideration had of the poore condition of John Elliat of Mitchell Creech who hath beene a souldier in the parliament service ever since theis late wars and hath received sever-all dangerous wounds in his body to his greate dis-tresse for want of a place of habitation he havinge a wife and twoe small children and the said John Elliat havinge gotten approbation both of the trustees of Mr Cuffe, Lord of the Manor, alsoe of the inhabitants of the said Parish for the erecting of a house for himselfe, for his wife Grace, for her life. It is assented unto and ordered by this court that the said John Elliat shall have liberty to erect and build a cottage on the said waste ground for the habitation of himselfe and family and after-wards the same shall be converted to the use of other poore people of the said parish of Michell Creech and shall be there placed in accordance to the statute in this behalfe made and provided.

1611
A humble petition before the Justices at Taunton John Bearde of Michell Creek, blacksmythe, who after having bought a small cottage and had in the new building thereof sett upp the same to keepe yo said supplicant his wife and children from wind and raine and blustros weather Ytt pleased God by fyer to distroy the same about seven daise sithence and like to have burned yore supplicants poore children as they laye in their beds had not yore said supplicant adventured his life beinge in great distresse to free them from fier. (An order was made for the petitioner to have £5 out of hospital money).

REMOVAL ORDER

Whereas John Stacey together with his wife and one child was apprehended in the Parish of Thame in the County of Berks. Aforesaid as a rogue and vagabond videlict as begging for alms and upon examination of the said vagabond taken before me, J.P. Andrews Esq. One of his Majesties Justice of Peace in and for the said County of Berks., Upon oath... it does appear his settlement is in the parish of Creech St Michael in Somerset.

A constable was required to take the vagabond to the Wiltshire border and hand him over to be taken to Somerset with his pass. There were many more instances of families being returned to their parish of settlement, and to be able to travel legally, a pass was required. Hence the records of the church show money handed and shelter given to those with an official pass 'paid unto a man his wife and two chil-dren for quarters for them one night having a lawful passe.' Also: 'Unto Mary Stevens and her mother and daughter who lay here from Saturday night till Sunday morning having a passe to travel to Ireland.'

BASTARDY ORDERS

So that a parish should not be responsible for children born out of wedlock, finding the man responsible was important. He could then be made to maintain the child until the point at which the courts decided that the child could be apprenticed if necessary. The following is a bastardy order from 1683:

By the order of Nathaniel Palmer and Richard Crosse Esquire, two of his Majesties Justice of Peace and quorum within the said county and ward adjoining the parish church of Michael Creech, in the same county made for the ----- of the said parish, and for the maintenance keeping and duration of Hannah, a bastard female child born of the body of Elizabeth Collins of the same widow and there now living and charged to be begotten by one Henry Collins of the same parish, yeoman, as follows.... Impris on examination of the said Elizabeth Collins only before one taken on oath we find Henry Collins is charged to have the oft and carnall knowledge of her body diverse times shortly after Easter in the year 1683 and that she chargeth him upon her oath to be the only ffather of the same child, whereupon we do order and adjudge him the said Henry Collins to be the reputed ffather of the same child and further orders followeth:

That the said Elizabeth Collins shall with the weekly pay hereafter appraised to keep and maintaine her said child untille it shall attaine the full age of eight years.

That the said Henry Collins shall from the birth of the said child, pay unto the overseer of the poore in the parish of Michael Creech for the tyme being and to their successors the sume of twelve pence weekly to be paid monthly every year toward the maintenance and keeping of the said child until it shall attain an age of eight [at which time it would then be apprenticed and no longer dependant on the parish].

A typical farm labourer's cottage. Three walls were cob and the side wall where the chimney was built would be brick.

Page from the baptism register 1835 showing entry of the children born out of wedlock. Girls were entered as 'natural', and boys as bastards or base born. Some vicars entered the names then scored them through.

There followed a long declaration that Henry Collins should give security to the overseers that he would abide by the decision, and the declaration ended; 'given under our hands and soules this first day of July Anno Regis 1684.'

Each order contained similar words, and over the next 150 years, many of these orders for the parish were recorded. In 1831, a certain boatman, James Laveridge, became responsible for two bastard children by the same woman, and she, six years later, had yet another child with a different father. In another case, the mother had to go to the house of correction and the supposed father went free.

The determination of the overseers not to pay for people when they felt it was not necessary is shown in the way they pursued the supposed fathers or runaways, and sent constables to bring them back to stand responsible for their misdeeds.

A child born within a marriage took its father's place of settlement, but a child born out of wedlock had to be settled in its parish of birth, hence the overseers' and churchwardens' eagerness to move a pregnant woman on to another parish.

BASTARDY ORDERS

1827
Margaret Pococke a bastard child, James Laveridge, boatman, the father:
1s.6d. for maintenance
14s. for apprehending him
12s. for the overseer.

1831
Margaret Pococke, male child,
James Laveridge, the father
£1.00 for the birthing
£1.00 for securing the father
10s. for filation order
8s.6d. maintenance (at 1s.6d. a week).

1837
Margaret Pococke, a male child, George Dyer, butcher, father.

The records from the Vestry meetings mention the poor children of the parish. In 1818 we read:

It was decided by principle of the inhabitants of this Parish that the churchwardens and overseers should cause to have vaccinated all poor children belonging to the parish whose parents [are] considered by them incapable of paying the expense themselves.

In 1834 it was agreed at the Vestry meeting that 'this day the poor shall be paid half the money and the other half in bread and the necessities of life.' In 1836 we read:

It is agreed at the Vestry meeting this day to borrow a certain sum of money toward the erection of a workhouse and the purchasing of land for the same as required by the Board of Guardians under the new Poor Laws.

The churchwardens approached Mrs Love Darbie and:

... negotiations for the purchase of the New Inn and Ship Inn (adjoining) with garden, orchard and other places thereunto belonging for turning into a workhouse for the keeping of the poor of the parish at such time and in such manner the publick house now being therein be put down as soon as possible.

But Mrs Love Darbie, who lived in Coal Harbour, Ham, did not want to sell the New Inn. Opposition to the removal of a local inn, which had stood on the site since early times, must have been quite strong. Perhaps its vicinity close to the church (and records show it was sometimes a disorderly house), made the churchwardens look for a good reason to have it removed. It still stands on its original site, so we presume that they were disappointed and that the workhouse was never built.

In 1799 money was paid to poor or out-of-work people to catch sparrows, as the churchwardens accounts show.

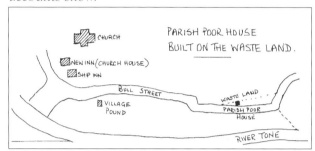

Above: *On the Tithe Map, numbers 276 and 277 were listed as the Poor House and garden, and two dwellings in Bull Street. These plots were owned by the parish officers, obviously as homes for the poor of Creech. The house designated for this purpose remains and is now called Sunnyside.*

Below: *The New Inn on the site of the old Church House, in the 1950s before it became The Riverside.*

MILITIA

In 1118 Henry II had started a system of enrolment of men for the militia, instructing them to have certain armour according to means as an insurance against invasion. This system remained in being for many years and, in 1569, the list for Creech was as follows:

Thomas Bobbet	light horseman
Thomas Burrowe	archer
Richard Upham	pekeman
John Godwin	billman
John Richard	pekeman
Nicholas Richard	archer
Richard Crosse	pekeman
Alex Crosse	archer
Thomas Beare	pekeman
Richard Bond	billman
Richd Bond	light horseman
John Bonde	billman
Wm Hayes	archer
John Hoper	archer
Wm Murley	billman
Richd Mogge	billman
John Lambert	billman
John Longe	archer
Wm Webber	archer
Wm Yevens	billman
Rbt Richardes	archer
Roger Mason	archer
Thomas Tymell	billman
Wm Oliver	billman
Walter Capper	archer
Robt Bailey	billman
John Stronge	archer

Enlisted men were paid one shilling and expected to be on call for six months. They would be paid conduct money to get to the place of muster.

An idea of the armour worn is given by the following brief accounts:

Robert Cuffe Esq. A corslet furnished ij calivers and 1 gelding for a light horseman furnished.
Alex Siddenham Esq. A gelding for a light horseman furnished.
John Crosse vj pair of almain rivets furnished.
Thos. Hannynge with swords and daggers ij bows.
Will Hayball iiij sheafs of arrows and ij bills and others.

The following note appears in October 1781:

TO THE CHURCHWARDENS OF THE PARISH OF CREECH ST MICHAEL.

Whereas John Beale of the Parish of Creech St Michael aforesaid hath been chosen by lot in the militia of this county before as his Majesties Deputy Lieutenant of Justice for the said county and hath provided John Giles of Columpton, labourer as his 'substitute' who has been sworn and enrolled to serve in the militia for three years, according to the Act of Parliament in that behalf made. These are therefore to require you to pay unto the said John Beale on sight thereof, the sum of four guineas which we do hereby adjudge to be one half of the current price paid to a volunteer according to the directions of an Act of Parliament, in that case made and provided given under the hands of this 10th of October 1781.
This is to certify that the above named John Giles is approved and now actually serving as a privateman in the Somerset Regiment Militia.

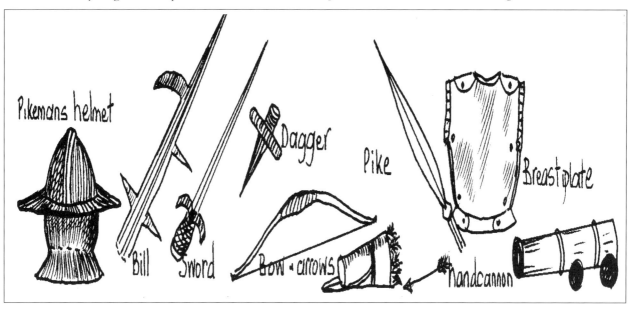

THE ANCIENT ORDER OF SHEPHERDS

In 1707 it was a common complaint from the established craft guilds that groups (such as the weavers) had formed clubs with a common seal, tipstaff and colours. Despite these grumblings, the new clubs began to increase in strength and their aim was to help those in need. Very strong in agricultural areas, Friendly Societies, as they became, brought great benefits to the communities which they served.

One such society existed in the parish of Creech and served Thurloxton, Lyng, West Monkton, Durston, Ruishton, Thornfalcon, North Curry, West Hatch, North Petherton and Stoke St Mary. This was a wide area, unusual for such a society. The Bell Inn at Creech was the headquarters. In 1787 the rules and regulations of Creech St Michael Friendly Society were published and the brass-headed pole, which was to be carried in ceremonial marches, was shown. This was made at a foundry in Bridgwater.

The actual distribution of money to the needy was carried out by special members called stewards, and they needed to see a certificate for those who were sick before money could be made available. The certificate had to be signed by a doctor, clergyman or overseer. Provision was made for those incapacitated by sickness or age, the fatherless, widows and for funeral expenses. The Creech Society was well known for its generosity, and many can still remember the comfort it brought to people.

The main event of the year was Whitsun, when the entire village had a day off – for some farm labourers often the only holiday they had. The day began with a church service, after which 3d. pieces were thrown to the children in the churchyard. One villager remembers scrabbling among gravestones for coins.

Everyone then proceeded through the village, led by the village band with the Society's banner held high. The brass pole was carried in the procession by a leading member in ceremonial dress and everyone wore their best clothes. The venue for the fair and feast varied, sometimes being enjoyed by the river bridge or where Rocketts Cottages now stand, but most often in the Bell Inn paddock. There would be a dinner for the men and a picnic for the rest, which would be followed by games and sports. The special day was abandoned during the Second World War.

The rules of the Society of the Ancient Order of Shepherds, as the Friendly Society was known, included the following:

A member must not join until 45 years old.
A member must not join with a secret illness.
The Society must meet quarterly.
If sick in another parish a certificate must be produced.
Members must be excluded if they wilfully hurt another member.
Also to be excluded if committed murder or theft.
£5 to be paid to a widow on decease of a member.

APPRENTICESHIPS IN THE 1600s

Children of the poor within the parish were apprenticed to local land-owners so that the burden of keeping them would not be a cost on the rates. The children would be taught a trade or how to be a servant or maid, and some bastards or base born were as young as seven when apprenticed.

Life was not always kind to them, although their masters had to provide adequate food, clothing and shelter, and teach them a craft or trade. Runaways were advertised for in the paper and threats were made to those harbouring them as those who paid for them did not wish to see their assets disappear.

In 1672 'Elizabeth Stallenge was apprenticed to Edmund Bobbett in the second year of the reign of William and Mary.' In 1792 'John Wright was apprenticed to Elizabeth Burridge until he was 21 years old.' The overseers of the parish met regularly to bind those poor in the parish deemed ready. The lists appear regularly in the Vestry minutes alongside regulations for keeping a child until 21 years old:

It was agreed to bind George Handole apprentice to Thomas Wetch to show him the art of his business and to pay him £9 out of poor rates and to clothe him once in that term. If his eye should disable him from following his trade then the said Thomas Wetch is to pay back to the parish a proportional part of the said nine pounds at the commencement of his apprenticeship.

Between 1782 and 1788, 13 children were apprenticed by Board officers. Many of the names are later seen in the poor book. They include: 'Will Elsom to George Knight and Will Lyle', 'Betty Fogarty to George Coombes', 'Henry Baker to George Shepherd at Coal Harbour', 'Martha Hodder to Rev. and Mrs Thomas Exon', 'John Baker to Thomas Dyer at Court Barton' and 'Will Maylard to Miss Mary Bobbett'.

The record of what was expected of each apprentice is not mentioned, but the places they went to and what they ended up doing must have varied enormously. The overseers were not concerned once the burden was removed, but history tells us that many were just unpaid servants from a very young age.

The banner of the Ancient Order of Shepherds at an outdoor service in 1930.

The village band and admirers outside the Bell Inn, 1934.

WEADON'S CHARITY

John Weadon, by his will dated 18 August 1862, directed his executors:

... to purchase in the names of the Vicar and Churchwardens for the time being of the Parish of Creech St Michael £250.0s.3d. Consols (for which £233.15s.0d. was paid), and for the Vicar and Churchwardens on 24 December in every year divide amongst the poor in such proportions as the Vicar and Churchwardens or the majority of them think proper.

DOWLIN'S CHARITY

Jane Dowlin died in 1855 having bequeathed to trustees:

... a sum of £300... Consols (for which £275.3s. 1d. was paid), the annual income arising from which was to be paid among such poor persons of the parish as shall not be in receipt of parochial relief and in such proportions as the trustees think proper.

Both these charities are still in existence and are administered by the Parish Council and the church.

ANNE SEAGAR

By her will dated 7 November 1741 Anne Seagar:

Gave and devised the sum of 40 shillings to be paid yearly out of her long leasehold estate lying in the Parish of Creech to be applied and disposed according to the discretion of the minister of the Parish for the time being, and her executors therein after named and his representatives for the keeping of five or more poor children of the said Parish at school to be taught to read and be instructed in church catechism.

The property in the said will has come by purchase to one Thomas Dyer, who bought it subject to the charge. The owner of the property has always paid the annual sum to the schoolmaster in the village and sent children to be educated by him.

Another sum of £1.00 is paid by the proprietor of a farm called Longellen (Mr Day), which he distributes himself among the poor. Of the origin of this gift, there is no trace within the parish.

HURLEY CHARITY

Very little is known of this charity. It is tied to a piece of land called Rowsells in Creech Heathfield, belonging to a Mr Hurley of Old Market Street, Bristol. It has been distributed for the last 40 years, but the present owner refused all information when the boards were tabulated in the Parish Church.

ADSBOROUGH PARISH ROOMS CHARITY 1916

The cottages from which the charity was paid were sold and the funds transferred to Creech Parish Church Organ Fund to pay an organist. Requests were made for the monies to go towards the organ fund itself but no proper deeds of the charity could be found.

All of these reports came from inspections of the Charities Commission over the years.

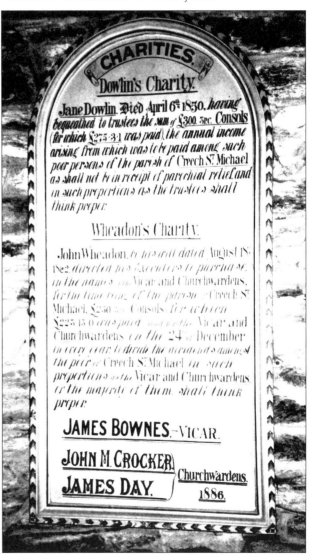

A plaque describing both Dowlin's Charity and Wheadon's Charity in the church.

Court Barton, the manor house of Creech St Michael. The present building was erected in 1633 on a much older site. Here the court leets were held.

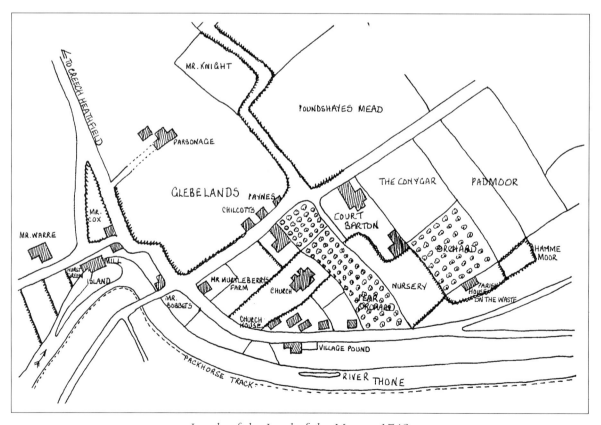

Lands of the Lord of the Manor, 1749

Chapter 4
Manor House, Taxes and Tithes

MANOR HOUSE OF CREECH ST MICHAEL

The Manor House of Creech St Michael has stood on the site since ancient times, and before the present building, a house of some kind is recorded on maps as a dotted area. The Cuffe family inhabited the house in 1535, when Anne Cuffe married Francis Warre of Hestercombe. The Cuffe tomb in the church is dated 1595. In a survey of the parish dated 1633, it is stated 'the village gives habitation to the Cuffes whose new house is its greatest ornament.'

The Cuffes were a widely distributed family, divided by the Civil War. James Cuffe was knighted by Charles II and given land in Ireland, while Thomas Cuffe, his father, had charge of a large division of the Parliamentary Army of Oliver Cromwell.

The estate agents in 1929 extolled the virtues of the property and described the rooms. Rumour had it that there was a secret passage from the church to the Manor, but it does have its own path to the north door. Some years ago, the descendants of the family came from America and contributed to the restoration of the Court Barton Chapel in the church.

At the Dissolution of the Monasteries in 1536, Creech was given to Thomas Wyatt, but he was accused of treason in 1554 and the Manor passed to Lord Hastings. Elizabeth I then gave it to the Cuffes in 1592, Robert Cuffe being a magistrate in Taunton.

During the 19th century the manor belonged to William Hussey of Salisbury. William Howard was the lord of the manor in 1861 (and his ancestors visited the area in 1991). In 1929 George Coombe sold the house to the Dunn family who then sold it to Dr Bowthorpe in the 1980s.

In 1901 Court Barton Estate was for sale and the accompanying statement extolled its virtues:

The Estate is situated in close proximity to the village of Creech St Michael. It adjoins good roads and is most accessible to the River Tone, Taunton and Bridgwater, the canal and good markets.

It occupies a warm sheltered position with an important advantage of a kindly goodworking deep loam soil on red gravel formation.

Possessing all the elements of active fertility, *essential for producing abundant crops of high class grain, roots and rich fattening pasture, and is deservedly famous as one of the earliest and Best farms in the neighbourhood. Where necessary, portions of the estate have been systematically drained. The meadow and pastures with well stocked and prolific orchards (forming a large part of the estate), are of extremely rich and valuable character, interspersed with abundant streams of warm spring water of great purity, greatly enhancing the value of the estate and justifying its being recommended to persons seeking a really sound and advantageous landed investment of a peculiarly profitable character.*

The social amenities and attractions of the neighbourhood are too well known to need more than a passing mention, and the beautiful scenery of the district with its healthful climatic advantages add additional charm to the property. A chapel or aisle in the church (30 sittings), belongs to the estate as the ancient courthouse and is now held and enjoyed therewith and there is a private entrance to the church.

HEARTH TAX, 1665

The Hearth Tax was a payment of 2 shillings to be made on every hearth 'in all houses paying to the church or poor.' Since Domesday, 'fumage or smoke farthing' had been paid, but this tax was to be properly registered and a record of each parish made (which gives us a good idea of how many houses there were in Creech at that time). It also recorded the number of hearths in each house and whether they were in use.

Naturally, some people would rather have gone cold than pay a tax to the king, so the records show that some houses had hearths which 'were now pulled downe', but it also showed those who were very poor and could not pay as 'not rated to church or poore for reasons of povertie.'

The largest number of hearths belonged to Edward Cely of Charlton, who had 20, and the vicar, Henry Masters, who had 10. Most people had 2 or 4. The tax was paid at Michaelmas and Lady Day.

COURT BARTON FARM,

situate in the Village of Creech St. Michael, adjoining the Church, comprising a

Fine Old Manor House,

AGRICULTURAL BUILDINGS, COTTAGES

and first-class well managed Meadow, Pasture, Orchard and Arable Lands in the occupation of Messrs. S. & G. Dunn on a yearly Michaelmas tenancy at the annual rent of

£465 11s. 0d.

and described as :—

Ord. No.	Description.			Quality.		Ordnance Area		
						A.	R.	P.
Pt. 148	Court Barton Residence, Grounds and Buildings			Homestead	...	2	0	20
Pt. 148	Churchyard Orchard	...	...	Orchard	...	0	2	14
Pt. 148	Canal Cottage and Garden	...	...	Buildings, etc.	...	0	0	35
131	Back Orchard	...	...	...	Orchard	...	1	3	32
Pt. 148	Cottage and Garden	...	...	...	Buildings, etc.	...	0	1	19
130, 129	Two and Three Acres or Second Field		...	Pasture, etc.	...	5	1	28
128	Nine Acres	...	...	...	Pasture	...	8	0	35
152	Little and Great Long Ash	...	...	Pasture	...	10	1	13
153	Maylors and Wilcox's Meadow	...	...	Meadow	...	7	2	7
Pt. 134	Entrance Road	...	...	...	Road	...	0	0	22
381	Eastern Coppice	...	..	...	Arable	...	4	2	7
380	Wheathills	...	...	...	Arable	...	6	0	6
374	Woodlands and Creech Wood	...	...	Arable	...	19	2	16
340	Western Coppice	...	..	...	Arable	...	5	1	36
339	Little and Great Wood Meads	...	...	Meadow	...	6	3	15
338	Foxhole Meadow	...	...	...	Meadow	...	7	3	6
337	Creech Wood	...	...	...	Arable	...	14	0	29
285	Groves and Bridge Three Acres	...	...	Arable	...	19	0	28
Pt. 162	Wrides Ground, etc.	...	...	Arable	...	5	3	32
284	Part Groves Orchard	...	...	Orchard	...	3	0	1
288	Part Thornibier Four Acres	...	...	Arable	...	2	0	13
292	Part Balls Meadow and Sharp Lands	...	Meadow	...	3	1	23
286	Part Balls Meadow, etc.	...	...	Pasture	...	7	1	31
161	Part Calf Hay, Sharphams, etc.	...	...	Meadow	...	12	1	36
150	Butt Paddock, etc.	...	...	...	Pasture	...	2	1	24
151	Part Horsecroft, etc.	...	...	...	Pasture	...	6	1	15
138	Part Poundhayes	...	...	...	Pasture	...	4	0	3
132	Coneygar	...	...	...	Pasture	...	2	2	1
					A.	170	0	27

The Residence

formerly the Court House of the Manor. is substantially built of brick and stone and has slated roof.

It contains the following :—ENTRANCE HALL, DRAWING ROOM, DINING ROOM, BREAKFAST ROOM, EIGHT BEDROOMS, Bath Room, Lavatory, best and secondary Stairs, Kitchens, Dairy, Cellars, Coal House and other Domestic Offices.

The Agricultural Buildings

include Cart Horse Stable, Hack Stable, Loose Boxes, Coachhouse or Garage, Wagon houses, Cider House with apple loft, Chaff house, Barn, Implement Shed, Cow stalls, Granary, Piggeries, Bartons and Yards.

The greater part of the Farm is free from Ecclesiastical Tithes and the Lay Tithes on a portion of the property belong to the Owners and are included in the Sale.

Outgoings : Apportioned Lay Tithes £2 18s. 0d.
Land Tax ... £11 17s. 11d.
Special Drainage Rates £1 16s. 11d.
Lord's Rent ... £10 11s. 2d.
Education Rent ... £2 0s. 0d.

Another view of Court Barton. The manor house was a farm for many years and it is now the home of Dr Bowthorpe and his family who have revealed some of the building's original features.

WINDOW TAX, 1671

The tax on windows was again seen as an imposition, and many householders closed up windows to avoid payment. The Celys of Charlton closed every second upstairs window and this remains so today. Strangely, any window in a dairy was exempt, so many windows had 'dairy' written over them.

The following entries appear in the Creech rates book during the 18th century: in 1761: 'James Muttlebury account for making the land tax and the window tax 7sh 6d.', and in 1763 'Hugh Collard account for work done about Ham Bridge and for settling the window tax and land tax.'

TITHES OF CREECH ST MICHAEL

In 787, King Offa made compulsory tithes or taxes to be paid based on a tenth or tithe of each person's property, whether it was land, crops or buildings, or a place of trade such as a mill. These tithes, paid to the Church or the lord of the manor, were for the upkeep of the building and all that it entailed. They were divided into great and small tithes, the first being corn, hay or wood, and the latter being other commodities. In later years these tithes were considered a hindrance to agricultural progress, for if a farmer improved stock or bought more land, his tithe payments would increase.

The surviving records of tithe payments provide an insight into the land in the parish, the seasonal variation of crops, the weather and any disputes arising, as in the grist mill at Ham.

Late-18th century records show the variety of goods involved in the payment of tithes:

1794-8
Hogshead of cyder from the orchard at the Glebe 12s.6d.
Hay from the orchard – an indifferent crop.
190 bushells of wheat.
152 bushells of barley.
Peas, beans and straw.
For a tithe pig.
An acre of potatoes.
A parcel of dung supposed 30 loads.
A tithe sheep and fat beasts.
The fall of a colt.

1795
10 hogshead of cyder.
Two milk cows, wool and the fall of a colt.

1796
Mary Arundell paid tithes in wool 43 lambs and apples.
Rec. from Mr Woodwards orchard, 2 bags of apples.

Impression of how Coal Harbour and Ham Mill might have looked around the middle of the 19th century. (© Tony Haskell)

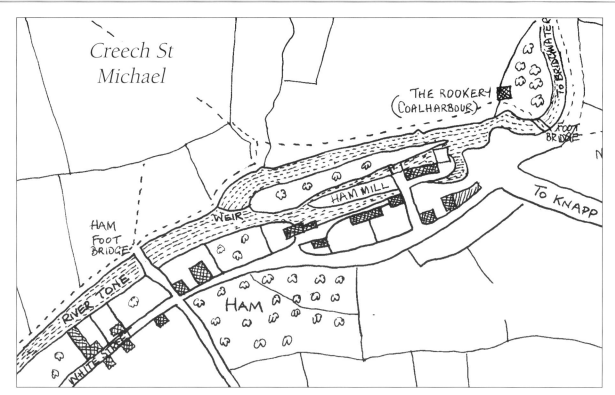

Map of Ham Mill in the 1950s.

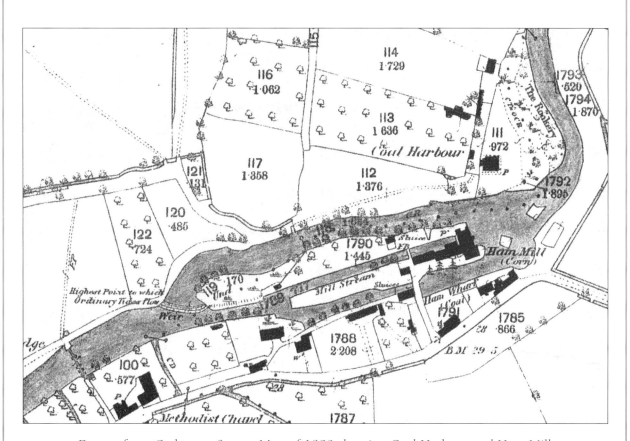

Extract from Ordnance Survey Map of 1889 showing Coal Harbour and Ham Mill.

Ham Mill, c.1890. The barges to Taunton used the cut in the foreground. The photographer put his bowler hat on the wall before taking this photograph! (Courtesy Margaret Adams, Creech St Michael)

1798
Field of grass belonging to Murtlebury (2 asses on it).
Blacksmith paid half a crown for fall of a colt.

In 1800 the vicar, Thomas Comber, recorded that 'it was a very scant harvest and crops were bad, being the amount of bushels was less than ever before since I came to Creech.'

After 1802 the tithes listed included chickens, potatoes, flax, geese, lambs, grey and white peas, beans and apples. Also, labour was mentioned, including hoeing, reaping and mowing.

The tithe map of 1837 shows all of the land-owners in the parish, the fields which they owned and the field numbers. Accompanying this map is a list of tithes due from each person. The imposition of tithes gave rise to a verse:

> *We've cheated the parson.*
> *We'll cheat him again.*
> *Why should the vicar have one in ten?*
> *One in ten, one in ten,*
> *Why should the vicar have one in ten?*

HAM MILL ON THE RIVER TONE

In the 1780s Will Manning withheld the tithes of Ham Grist Mill for which he was summoned to court. He alleged:

... the Grist Mill is a very ancient mill and was erected before the ninth year of the reign of Edward II, some time King of England, and had never paid tythes to the said Thomas Exon (vicar of Creech St Michael), or his predecessors. That the Grist Mill was part of the demesne land of the ancient prior of the Convent of Montacute of the Order of Cluniac Monks in the Diocese of Bath and Wells, and that by ordination or endorsement of the Vicarage of Creech St Michael bearing the date of 20th day of October 1362, made by Ralph Lord Bishop of Bath and Wells.

He continued 'that the ordained vicar should have tythes, except those of the above demesne', and went on to state that the mill, being part of the demesne, had never paid tythes. The court decided in favour of Will Manning and Thomas Exon paid all the dues of the court case.

Chapter 5
Vicars and Churchwardens

The incumbent was an important figure throughout the history of a parish. His duties outside church services varied, but he was considered very necessary to the wellbeing of life within a parish. He was required to certify public punishment or testify to a person's character. As well as conducting baptisms, marriages and burials, he was Chairman of the Vestry meetings and was in overall charge of church and parish affairs. He had certain rights of tithes, and, as previously mentioned, the records kept of those tithes over the years are a source of information on crops and harvests at that time.

In 1362 a record of the entitlement of the vicar to tithes reads:

The vicar should have parsonage house with orchards and gardens belonging there unto also arable and pastureland of the said parsonage, but 7 acres of arable and pasture for 8 oxen must go to Montacute. The vicar shall also have tithes of hay, wool, milk, mills, fisheries and all small tithes of whatsoever except those which appertained to the Priory. Likewise, one third of all tithes of corn and commanage in the parish, half a mark must go to Wells and 40 pence to Taunton.

The entries in the tithe book from 1797 state the kind of produce paid to the church in tithes. These include: cows, wool, apples, cider, wheat, barley, peas, beans, straw, fat, beasts, lambs and a 'fall of a colt.'

In 1800 it is recorded by Thomas Comber, the vicar:

Wheat sold at 18s. per bushel, but owing to a very scanty harvest and being a bad crop, the amount of number of bushels was less than ever before I came to Creech.

In 1805 the record reads:

The apples grown in the orchards on the Vicarage lands made upwards of 14 hogshead of prime cyder worth at Christmas £3.3s. per hogshead (42 guineas), and 1 hogshead of watery cyder worth 2gns for the trouble of making the same.

Visitations to the church from the Bishop would sometimes, in the reports, mention the failings of the incumbent - as in 1603, when it was curtly observed that: 'the Rev. Mailer is no preacher.'

In 1922 the parish and the vicar were in disharmony over the war memorial being outside the churchyard, and much angry discussion took place, but it was not until the 1970s that the memorial was placed inside the churchyard.

West door of the church. The niches on either side once held statues.

Vicars of the Parish of Creech St Michael from 1318

? Thomas   1318
W. De Bokland   1320
W. De Hornley   1327
C. De Shepton   1327
J. De Borthon   1353
E. Barlinch   1364
W. Weston   1412
R. Gosse   1427
R. Maister   1432
J. Tonker   1456
J. Crook   1457
C. Sydenham   1490
W. Vincent   1524
J. Gore   1546
D. Mailer   1556
D. Mailer   1575
T. Mailer   1627
H. Masters   1641
deposed during commonwealth
T. Batt   1651
H. Masters reinstated   1662
J. Gale   1666
W. Mitchell   1696
F Archer   1702
J. Gale   1704
W. Skarret   1738
T. Exon   1781
T. Tomber   1806
J. Cresswell   1813
J. Ostrehan   1851
S. Morgan   1871
J. Bownes   1877
W. Shillito   1901
M. Colby   1931
W. Morris   1945
R. Whitwell   1948
R. Holmes   1956
K. Jones   1965
D. Manning   1992

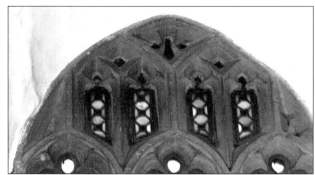

Above and right: *A small area of medieval glass in the oldest part of the church.*

Edmund Barlynch was at the centre of a disagreement when the Archbishop of Taunton refused to induct him as vicar of Creech in 1364, so the Prior of Montacute, Brother Gerald, instructed the rector of West Monkton and the vicar of Wynford to induct him.

David Marler died in 1627 and is buried under the communion table, as also are John Gale and his son, both vicars of the parish.

There is a tablet on the wall recording the death of Thomas Exon and his son, also Thomas, who died aged 14 years from a fall from a horse in 1792. An Exon was involved in the Monmouth Rebellion but was not 'taken'.

The Reverend Osternan was in office until 1870 and he was the son of Joseph of Barbados.

From 1490 to 1524 Sydenham (of Combe Sydenham) was the vicar. He had been a student at Oxford and a rector of a Cornish church. He rarely took a church service, leaving it to his curates and he was also seldom seen in the parish, being too busy with other affairs.

Combe Sydenham

CHURCHWARDENS

Known as the Proper Guardians or Keepers of the Parish, the wardens had many responsibilities. They would be required to keep account of the expenses of the church, and to ensure the laws of the church were adhered to regarding property.

In 1552 the law decreed that every parish should have a strong wooden chest with a hole in the top and three strong keys in which to keep the alms for the poor. Later this became the receptacle for books of christenings, marriages and burials and was known as the parish chest. The churchwarden's job was to maintain this and it was a very important part of the furnishings of the church. The churchwardens' accounts of the parish were well kept and we can read them today. They give us a fascinating glimpse of the everyday life in the parish.

Money would be spent on candles and tallow for lighting, books, bells, clocks and maintenance fees. The wardens kept account of the salary of the clerks, gifts to singers, visitations, church bellringers and such tasks as the cleaning of the church.

An Act of 1553 stated that the duties of the churchwarden must include the eradication of 'noylfull fowles and vermyn.' The account books show money paid to 'Chappells boy for killing a hidgehog', a similar sum 'Paid Edmund Chapell for killing a polecat' and also money 'Paid for killing a fox.'

A dog whipper was paid to rid the church of nuisance dogs. Sheep dogs and turnspit dogs could accompany their masters to church but other dogs were removed - sometimes with wooden tongs for safety.

Later, churchwardens were responsible for keeping account of settlement orders. Constables would be sent from other parishes to accompany or collect those being returned to their place of birth so that the parish did not become responsible for the cost of strangers.

The churchwarden originated as a representative of his church and was answerable to the Bishop on affairs of the parish. In medieval times it was a very important position, covering all manner of duties and, because of this, more than one churchwarden would be appointed, as in 1787 when James Dean and Hugh Collard filled the posts. Again, in 1835, John Bucknell and John Godfrey shared the position.

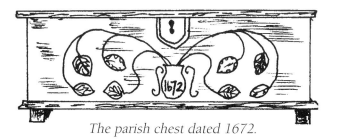

The parish chest dated 1672.

EXTRACTS FROM THE CHURCHWARDENS' ACCOUNTS, 1666–94

Paid out to Henry Chappell for a ladder to go to the top of the tower 1s.
Paid unto a man that bought from London a book to be published in the church 6d.
Laid out for the hospital and maimed soldiers 19s.6d.

1667
Gave soldiers returned ffrom Holland 6d.
Paid 4 seamen being redeemed ffrom Hollanders 6d.
Paid for ye washing of ye surplices 1s.
Paid Edmund Bobbetts man for killing a fox 4d.
Paid Edmund Bobbetts man for killing a polecat 4d.
Gave a poore man, his wife and 2 children four quarters for them one night having a lawfull passe 1s.2d.
Gave 2 poore men one of them burnt by fyre 1s.

1674
Paid to Thomas Norman for beinge a poore man 2d.
Paid unto a company of travellers numbering 12 who hath greate losse by fyre travelling to Ireland 1s.2d.
Gave to ye ringers 29th of May being His Majesties Birthday and his happy restoration 1s.
Paid unto Will. Chappell for ringing the great bell Jan.30th being the day His Majesty was put to death 1s.

1688
Paid John Chappells boy for killing 3 hidgehogs 6d.
Beere for ye ringers when the Prince of Wales was born 3s.6d.
For my expenses on the day of Thanksgiving for the coming of Their Majesties and the delivering of the nation from popery and slavery Beere for ye ringers when tidings of a greate fight at sea and victory over the French 6d.

1694
To Will Bonan and Thos. Alford for hanging the great bell when it was fallen down 12s.
For the thousand and quarter of nails 2s.1d.
For killing an otter 1s.
For a poste to hang ye church hatts 2s.
For eleven sacks of lyme 11s.

Parish Church, early 1900s.

Creech Parish Church before the stained-glass window dedicated to the Revd Bownes was installed behind the altar.

Chapter 6
Church and Chapel

CREECH ST MICHAEL PARISH CHURCH

The oldest part of the church, built in the 13th century by the Cluniac Monks of Montacute, is the North East Chapel, now happily restored to make a place for quiet prayer. There are small fragments of medieval glass in the north window, and a remnant of ancient floor tile on the floor. In this chapel is the once brightly-coloured Cuffe tomb, still a special feature of the Court Barton Chapel.

The north and south doors are typically 13th century, made of thick oak planks fastened by wrought-iron nails driven in then bent over. These doors were opened on special occasions so that the congregation could parade all through the church. At a christening the north door was opened to let out the devil.

Under the west window the gallery stands with its coat of arms of Queen Anne. The gallery was built in 1826, and the churchwardens record that 'Mr Beadon Newton's pew was disturbed by the construction.' There was a system of pew renting in church and this accounts for the concern of the churchwardens at this 'disturbance'.

The gallery was for musicians as the church did not have an organ (this came 22 years later). It is interesting to see the school today on festive occasions use the area as of old.

The arms of Charles I are displayed on the north wall. Parishes displayed coats of arms as a sign of loyalty to the monarch.

The nave was once adorned with wall paintings, some of which have been partly restored. As most medieval worshippers were illiterate, these bright images enhanced the teachings of the church. At the Reformation they were covered over and only revealed in recent years. A full restoration would be interesting but at the time of writing has not been attempted.

High on the wall of the chancel to the left is a small opening from a tiny gallery. The staircase to this still exists but is inaccessible. This small opening indicates that a galleried rood screen once stood at the entrance to the chancel. Rood screens protected the priest from the congregation and scavenging dogs. Part of this screen was still in place in the early 1900s as old photographs show.

Each chapel had its rood screen so that the families who endowed them were able to worship in private. The North Chapel was used by the inhabitants of Court Barton, and a pathway from the house to the church allowed them to keep their distance from the rest of the congregation.

Across the aisle is the Charlton Chapel, which was maintained by the Pocockes and Cely families, who all lived at Charlton. The coat of arms on the wall is of the Cely-Trevillion family. The Celys' were joined in marriage to the Trevillions' of Middleney, Curry Rivel. The ceiling in the chapel is similar to the ones in Court Barton and Coal Harbour. On the floors of the chapels are the memorial tablets of the inhabitants of those houses, which are dated from the early years of the church. Memorials to past vicars, wealthier parishioners and people whose lives touched the community of Creech in the past but were not prominent in the records, can also be found throughout the church.

At the back of the church the Muttlebury family, who farmed around the church and who gave land in order to extend the churchyard, have their commemorative tablets.

The Savidge family, brick-makers both in the village and in Bridgwater (Elizabeth Savidge married John Board of Bridgwater), have a family memorial by the south door, and the Keyte stone to the right of the altar is to one of the lords of the manor.

The porch was a most important place where meetings were held, women churched after childbirth, records kept in the parish chest (dated 1672), business transacted and, when a threat of war was imminent, arms were stored. The list of incumbents since 1318 is recorded on the wall, as are two charities for the relief of the poor dated 1866.

Outside the south door is a scratch sundial, which would tell any latecomer to a service exactly how late they were! On the west font can be seen 'mask corbiels', carved by local masons to represent parishioners. In niches both inside and outside the church stood statues, removed at the Reformation. The north side of the church is where, according to

The stocks in the churchyard.

Ancient yew and stocks with the photographer, the figure in the picture.

superstition, the devil dwelt, so strangers, plague victims and criminals were buried there. Also on this side of the church are the steps to the tower where for centuries ringers have climbed to the bell tower to summon people to church or celebrate special occasions.

The waggon roof of the church, with its shape resembling a covered wagon, was probably carved by a local craftsman. Its lustre faded over the years but in 1973 a local carpenter, C. Bryant, repaired parts of the roof and re-gilded the bosses. The octagonal font is 14th century but the carved cover is Victorian.

The ancient yew is reputed to be 1000 years old, planted perhaps before the first stone church. Its branches were used to decorate the church and line coffins, and its poisonous berries served to deter cattle from grazing in the churchyard. Under the tree are the village stocks where troublemakers and law breakers were imprisoned for periods commensurate with the crime. The outer walls of the churchyard have initials set into them at intervals, and these refer to an ancient custom, possibly unique, of wall work tenements which was long ago recorded as follows:

... there was an immemorial usage or custom within the said parish of Creech St Michael, whereby certain persons, owners of messuages or tenements and ancient enclosed lands had always been liable to maintain and repair... certain respective portions of the wall or fence around the churchyard of the parish of Creech, aforesaid commonly called wallworks, and in right of common equal in number to the number recorded by certain initials on several distinct departments of the wall.

Some 111 of these initials were recorded of which 23 can still be seen but another 11 are indecipherable.

Top: *The font decorated for the Flower Festival in the church, 1990s.*

Above: *One of the still visible sets of initials carved into the churchyard wall.*

Left: *The coat of arms of the Cuffes on the tomb of Robert Cuffe, 1593.*

Right: *Corbel on the church wall.*

THE CHURCH IN THE MIDDLE AGES

Everyone in the parish was expected to attend church three times on Sundays, and it was a far different place than we see today. There were few seats, no hymns, rarely a sermon and if there were books, hardly anyone could read. People wandered about chatting and joking and as one writer said: 'gave each other the glad eye, lolling against the pillars and arguing.' This does not imply that people did not regard religion as important, rather that it was a part of everyday life.

When Revd de Shepton was the incumbent in the 1350s, he wrote that the parishioners found it difficult to attend daily services and sometimes he said Mass alone. A law in 1355 directed that a man must worship in his own parish, and the vicar of St Mary's in Taunton was told to look at his congregation, and if he saw anyone from another parish he must expel them. In Revd Sydenham's time, the church became a more sacred place so people met outside the church in a room close by (now the Riverside Inn). Here the villagers would gather and decide how to make money to support the church. Church ales were held and beer was brewed to sell.

As the church was no longer a place for festivals and merrymaking, it was decided to put in seats and a pulpit as preaching was becoming more popular. The church interior was quite bright with painted screens and wall pictures to assist a mainly illiterate congregation to understand stories from the Bible.

REFORMATION

Life in the parish changed again as Henry VIII broke away from the Church of Rome and installed himself as head of the Church of England. Parishes began to plan their own religious services. Each church was given a Bible in English, 'For every man that shall look and read thereon.' These were expensive and sometimes chained to the church. Parish registers had to be kept to record baptisms, marriages and deaths, and the priest had to ensure that the congregation knew the Lord's Prayer, the Ten Commandments and the Articles of Faith. If the vicar was absent he had to make certain that he had a replacement to take the service (I wonder how the services went before this!).

When Henry VIII died in 1547, young Edward VII came to the throne and things changed again. Revd Gore had to supervise the abolition of candles at Candlemass, ashes on Ash Wednesday and palms on Palm Sunday, and he had to remove all images. The service had to be held in English and a prayer book was to be used. Stone altars were to be replaced by wooden tables and communicants were to have wine with the bread. Royal officials were appointed to record church plate, vestments and surplices. At this time, the walls of the church were whitewashed to cover the paintings. In 1553, the fanatical Queen Mary Tudor came to power. She wanted churches to be refurbished, but parishes found it difficult to find the money so little was done.

All this change caused confusion in the parishes, but when Elizabeth became Queen in 1558 she reversed Mary's policies and established the Church of England, much as it is today. In 1604, Church leaders were worried about congregations as they felt the 'truly Godly' were in the minority and people attended church for a 'neighbourly gathering'. It was said that people were 'gazing about and never at the preacher'. One mention of services by a Westcountry girl included the following observation: 'such a bibble-babble that I am weary to heare yt, and I can sitt downe on my seate and take a napp.'

Left: *The Riverside Inn stands on the site of the Church House.*

Below: *One of the painted bosses in the church.*

The congregation arrived late and left early and failed to join in the psalms, whispering and joking and 'some stretched out to sleep.' One priest said the people found sermons beyond their comprehension, but he referred mainly to the poor, as the gentry yeomen and craftsmen seemed to fit in with Church ideals. During the Reformation visits were made to the church to see if rules were being obeyed:

1603
Visitation found the roof was in disrepair and windows. Reverend Mailer was no preacher and did not catecize.
1613
The chancel needed repairing. Three residents were excommunicated for non attendance at Easter.
1634
Another visitation – had no complaints.
1666
A list was made of church goods, it was recorded that there were no hymns or psalms and no organ.
1684
The bell fell down and was replaced at a cost of 12 shillings
1776
The church had 30 communicants and a small school

THE PARISH CHURCH IN RECENT TIMES

Recent times have seen just as much change in the life of the church. Perhaps some still stretch out to sleep or gaze about, but the atmosphere in our parish church is of a place well used and cared for, although with reminders of those far-off times when it was the very centre of parish life.

In the 1980s, the Church Council agreed to launch a restoration appeal. Surveyors had found serious movement of the south transept which was in urgent need of attention, and the gradual movement of the wall was having an effect on other parts of the church. In the meantime, the wall had to be shored up to prevent possible collapse.

The window glass, the tower and its louvred windows were also in need of repair. An estimated £20 000 was needed for immediate repairs, and the parish responded with enthusiasm – the remainder of the money being given over a longer period of time.

At the same time it was decided to remove the organ, which obliterated the Cuffe tomb, and move it further back in the north aisle. This revealed the oldest part of the church with medieval tiling and window glass.

Top: *Pew in the church.*
Above: *Vicar's reading desk dated 1634.*

One of the old wall paintings of Biblical texts above the gallery.

The church was limewashed at regular intervals probably to protect the soft stone.

CHURCH AND CHAPEL

THE BELLS

BELLS OF THE PARISH CHURCH

1. Ad Majoriem Die Glorium
DDWFS William Francis
2. Mrs Godfry Taunton (no date)
3. G P 'Halleluah' 1609
4. G P 'Praise Thee O God'
5. James Bownes, Vicar 1838 5 Alphabet
D M V 1590
6 'Drawe Nearer To God' G P I H 1614

The bells were a very important aspect of village life and were used to celebrate life and death. Tolling of the bell told the parishioners something of the deceased, it being rung nine times for the death of a man, six times for a woman and three for a child. This was followed by tolling the age of the deceased. On hearing the bells a person would say: 'When the bell begins to toll, Lord have mercy on the soul.'

The following references are made to the bells in the churchwardens' accounts:

1660
Gave ye ringers 29th of May being his Majesties birthday and his happy restoration.'
1676
Paid unto Will Chapple for ringing ye great bell Jan. 30th, being the day his Majesty was put to death.
1685
Paid Will Chapple for ringing the King's Knell.
1689
Beer for ye ringers when the Prince of Wales was born.
1691
Beer for ye ringers when the tidings of great fight at sea and victory over the French.

LIST OF CHURCH GOODS, 1661

1 Silver Chalice
Pulpit cushion
Chest trunk
1 Bible
2 Prayer Books
Hammer to mend the Bells

INVENTORY OF CHURCH PROPERTY, 1684

A greene cloth for ye communion table
One Holland table cloth for ye same
One silver challis with flagon
One book of homilies
One statute book
One church book of accounts
One iron frame for an hour glass
One leather box to put ye challis in
One glass bottle for wine
Mats to kneel on at ye communion
One new chest to put ornaments in
One great church Bible
Two books of common prayer for the minister and clerks to read
A surplice for ye Minister
One hammer to mend ye bells with

CHURCH MAINTENANCE

The following 19th-century records of church maintenance survive:

1826
There had been great work done in the church in with bills of £12, £4, £5, £5, £6 and £5.
Hannah Tarr was paid for cleaning the church 'after repairing.'
1828
5 bell ropes purchased
1831
New locks for the church coffers
1832
Paid Mr Kingsbury for two prayers
Paid for a base vile bow
Bill for repairing lead and glazing
A day's work for a man mowing the yard
For painting yard gates
2 hogshead of lime and carriage
49 sparrow heads at 2d. a dozen
Repairing the clock
For drawing
For 18 dozen sparrow heads at 2d. a dozen
1844
Paid a man to take ivy off the walls.
1845
False bottom to pulpit

In 1896 the *Taunton Courier* carried a report of a jumble sale in the village with a washing competition for ladies with prizes donated by Sunlight Soap. This raised £35, and the money was used to buy 15 lamps with 50 candle power, brass and 15 brass rod stands for the church, some of which remain to this day.

Reverend Golby dedicating the war memorial in 1922 with Vicarage Farm in the background.

Church choir, c.1930.

THE WAR MEMORIAL

The war memorial was situated opposite the road to Mill Row because the Reverend Golby was opposed to it being in the churchyard (see chapter 5). There was much village feeling about this, but in 1957 it was moved to the churchyard as building was planned for the site. The memorial was dedicated in 1922, and the names of those who died in the First World War were:

> ADAMS, JIM
> DART, WILLIAM
> DAY, ALEC
> DAY, GORDON
> HARVEY, GEORGE
> HILL, HERBERT
> HOOPER, JIM
> HOPKINS, CHARLIE
> MITCHELL, CHARLIE
> POOLE, GEORGE
> WEST, WILFRED

The Second World War names read:

> DUKE, M.
> LEDDINGTON, R.
> ROCKETT, J.L.
> THATCHER, G.R.
> VILE, E.C.
> WALSH, W.J.

Many of these families still live in the parish and can trace their relatives back several generations.

For the first Armistice celebrations, Mr Kingdon, the headmaster, arranged for the villagers and the schoolchildren to assemble around the War Memorial. The children whose fathers had died in the war laid wreaths and then the schoolchildren sang hymns. Miss Dunning, who had been associated with the school since 1873, expressed her appreciation of the beauty of the service and reverence of the children. Services were held every year at the memorial, led by members of The British Legion, and poppies and wreaths are now laid in the churchyard on the spot from where the memorial was removed.

Right top: *The war memorial placed inside the churchyard.*

Right: *When the war memorial was in its old position opposite Mill Row, the village schoolchildren decorated it with flowers. Mr Kingdon, the headmaster, being an ex-Army man, insisted that the children respect the occasion and behave impeccably.*

The chapel at Adsborough.

Village outing outisde the old Baptist chapel, 1934.

CREECH ST MICHAEL BAPTIST CHAPEL

In 1816, when Pig Barrel Lane was the main road through the village, John Rich registered a room in a house there for public religious worship. James Blatch Cox was associated with this and he later bought land from Francis Gale and the chapel was erected on the site. Before this, the land on which it stood was a farm where Methodist meetings were held.

In 1858 a vestry and schoolroom were added, but in 1884 they were demolished and a new school-room was opened by Mr Sommerville, the mill owner. In 1906 the chapel was used by the school-children for cookery lessons, and until 1973 was used as a hall for the school. In the 1980s the old building was demolished and the Zion Baptist Church was built.

A man named Gabriel was the pastor in 1830 and remained in the post until 'manifestations of unpleasant feeling' forced him away.

The Sunday School thrived at the chapel in the 1840s, and by the 1880s had 130 pupils and 10 teachers.

John Wesley is reputed to have preached in the parish on his tour of the area in 1754. He relates that he preached in Charlton and again a year later when he wrote: 'It rained, which lessened the congregation at Charleton.' The people came from a wide area to hear him and many land-owners protested. He again mentions Charlton in 1768 and 1770. Although there are several Charltons in Somerset, strong anecdotal evidence links John Wesley with Charlton in Creech.

In 1842 there was the Weslyan Chapel at Northend which closed in 1855, although it was still standing in 1876. In that year Methodists worshiped in a cottage in Creech Heathfield.

View of North End Creech St. Michael

THE SOCIETY OF FRIENDS IN CREECH.

This Society was quite strong in the parish in the 1600s, and records remain of meetings held in the village. They met in Cheads House, which stood where Cheads Cottages stand today at Northend. Friends met to discuss money for the poor, proposed marriages and problems of such unsociable vices as infidelity and drunkenness.

The following give a taste of items discussed at such meetings:

1676 Two shillings to be delivered unto Richard Plenty for the supply of Elizabeth Chappel, an ancient feeble woman standing in need of supply.

1677 Desired by Friends at this meeting that John Dobin, Thomas Burge and Philip Escwood to visit William Mitchell and speak to him concerning drunken and ill-behaviour, and that they should return and report to the meeting.

1681 It appearing to this meeting according to reference at last meeting in relation to a marriage proposed by Jonathan Allen betwixt him and Mary Hodge, that all things are clear and no cause or obstruction to hinder the intended marriage. This meeting doth confirm that the said partyes may be joined together in such convenience to them.

1687 Complaints were being made that Jonathan Allen of Creech, walked 'very dis orderly' being overcome with drunkenness to the great dishon-our of truth. This meeting orders that Will. Calbreath, John Powell, Will Chead and Thomas Buss, or any two of them do, in love to his soul, visit him and admonish him to disclaim himself from such wickedness and to give him account of this meeting.

(Later, Jonathan Allen acknowledged 'his being overtaken by drunkenness and did manifest his being sorry.').

1688 Jonathan Allen was found to be drunk and visited by Friends.

1691 Francis Scott was visited by Friends, regarding the taking up of arms in the time of the Monmouth Rebellion.

1709 Edmund Fry, after a visit from Friends 'did not refrain from his evil ways of spending his tyme extravagantly drinking'. So a testimony was drawn up 'to lett people know that the faithful Friends hath no unity with him.'

The Home Guard, Second World War. (Courtesy Ron Welch)

Left to right, back row: Messrs Pollard, Bill Hunt, Marc Marchant, Harold Wyatt, ? Cornwall, Bob Wheadon, Triss Foxwell, Norman Drewe, Ron Welch; middle: ? Cornwall, Mitchell, Bill Cruys, Fred Hunt, George Sandford, ? Hooper, Lance Coombes, Jack Taylor, Ivor Brookes, Harold Thomas, Jim Wadham; seated: Jack Sweeting, Rub Bauer, Perce Brookes, Cubby Bishop, Tacker Sweeting, Lieut Fisher, Ron Smith, Len Mitchell, Digger Wyatt, Brian Wakely.

Chapter 7
Law, Order and Conflict

PARISH CONSTABLES

During many centuries of English History, the constable has been responsible for law and order within the parishes. It is one of the oldest of the parochial services. Historians cannot agree on the year of the first record of a constable being appointed, but it seems likely to have been about 1200. His job was to ensure the parish armoury was stored and properly maintained, and the muster list up to date from 1400 to the 1600s. Until the end of the 16th century it was his responsibility to suppress beggars, lodge the poor, apprentice children and remove vagrants; this besides dealing with crime.

In 1833 William Paul and Richard Sharman were appointed as constables for the year ensuing, and were sworn into their respective offices within fifteen days, and in default, ammerced 'in the sum of five pounds each.' The following year William Coles and George Brass were sworn in as constables.

The Police House was at the cottage called Buckland, in Creech Heathfield, but this was replaced by a purpose-built house in the 1920s. The village policeman lived there and it was a substation with a blue light outside and information boards. Until 1994, PC Stocker was the parish constable and, with the help of Mrs Stocker, manned the station.

During the 1950s and '60s PC Dai Davis (also a rugby player) was a familiar figure at village events. His presence was a deterrent to the lads wanting to disrupt proceedings, but he knew everyone and was a well respected village constable. Tiny Weaver (who was not tiny), rode his motorbike around the parish for many years, and PC Osment, in the 1900s, is captured in village photographs 'keeping the noisy crowds at bay.' There were also several special constables in Creech. Now the parish is served by community policing centred at Taunton.

In 1869 William Sweeting was fined for allowing his donkey to stray in Ruishton, 6s.6d. and poaching was recorded in Creech. The following report was made:

Going up a lane in Creech, the defendant saw a man with a dog, a gun and a rabbit in his pocket. The defendant on whose land it was, demanded the rabbit. When the rabbit was given to him, the defendant hit him in the face with it. He threw the rabbit down and offered a fight, saying he would knock his eye out in one blow. Fined 10s. for poaching.

P.C. John Stocker was the parish policeman until 1994 when the service became centralised. At the time of writing he still lives at the Old Police House in Creech.

1640-59 ASSIZE COURTS

Upon reading the Petition of the inhabitants of Michell Creech in this county against Thomas Hooper of the said parish for the keeping of an inne there, frequently sufferinge many disorders, to be committed with this said house and especially on the Lords Day to the greate dishonour of Almighty God and the hindrance of His service, this court does desire the next Justice of Peace to Mitchell Creech aforesaid, upon sight of this order to grant a warrant for the apprehending of the said Thomas Hooper and to bind him at the next assizes and generalle goale deliver to beholden for this County there to be indicted and porceede according to lawe concerning these premises.

A record survives in the Archives Office which is dated 1659 of a 'Bond of 5 shillings 6d. bt. Thomas Hooper to churchwardens and overseers for distraint of goods'.

Sheep Stealing at Charlton Gate, 1668

The following account was filed based on the information of Will Joy of Thurloxton:

That yesterday in the morning he went to see a [?] sheepe he had on his ground and he found one of them was missing (being a white woather sheepe), and yesterday in ye afternoon a John Huton of [?] told this informant that he tooke up a sheepskin out of the River Tone at Charlton Gate. This informant said that the sheepskin bought him was the skin of the same woather sheepe which he had missed aforesaid, being marked with the owners mark upon. This produced a warrent to search the house of Robert Banfield at [?]. They found three joints of mutton, two legs one shoulder being hid. Then a head was produced torn by a dog, Robert Banfield kept a mastiff dogg. Edward Bellringer [was the] informant. Robert Banfield said he bought the sheepe from a butcher at Wellington. He was charged on suspicion of stealing the sheepe.

In 1673 the following appeared in the Records from the Taunton Assize Courts

Susanah Nott, wife of Thomas Nott of Creech St Michael, said her husband oftimes did abuse her and particular on Saturday last was, he fell upon her beating her with a staff he had in his hand about her shoulders and armes by which she was blodied on her nose and about her shoulders with the said beating. She said she lived in greate fear. He was warned about beating his wife and had to promise he would cease and she was told to return to him.

In 1876:

Richard Sidgewick of Creech St Michael was summoned on the complaint of Sergeant Goldsmith for selling on May 15th to Edward Coles, 2oz of coffee and 2oz of mustard as pure and unadulterated, whereas the same was there and then adulterated and impure. The purchases were analysed and provwn. The defendant said he knew the coffee was mixed with chicory but the mustard was as he bought it in Taunton. Fined 9s.6d.

In 1896 a case before the courts concerning a man from Creech whose wife was often drunk. It was stated that the wife was Irish and had 'lived quite a life'. The landlords of the pubs in the parish had refused to serve her. She had pawned the clothes, lit no fires and prepared no meals. The magistrate granted him a separation order. The chairman of the bench said he must be a respectable man 'being employed by G.W.R. Later the wife was in trouble again for being drunk on the highway, causing a cyclist to swerve and fall off his bike.

The following appeared in 1897 in the *Taunton Courier*:

A boatman at Creech was accused of stealing an eel spear, valued at £5. Police Constable Osment went along the canal and saw the defendant with an empty coal barge. Upon looking into the barge he saw an eel spear. Mr Bobbet said he had left the spear by his door but the defendant said that he had found it by the bridge. Thomas Virgin, a boatman for 20 years, said he knew the defendant and had seen him unloading slate from Bridgwater and Samuel Coles, the lad who drove the horses attached to the barge, said the defendant had walked to the bridge with him. The bench dismissed the case.

In 1898 the same paper reported the following case:

Frank Alway said he was going home when this man he had never seen before approached him and knocked him down twice. Joseph Adams gave evidence and said all three of them had left the pub at closing time under the influence of drink. They had all argued and hit each other. The case was dismissed with the bench adding that it was six of one and half a dozen of the other.

At the Courts, a case of misbehaviour of youths in the village when PC Osment had 'been disposed to conceal himself' led the Bench to say 'we wish Creech would, with the Jubillee in mind, provide recreation for the youths of the village.'

CREECH ST MICHAEL AND THE MONMOUTH REBELLION

Economic, political and religious problems which brought about the Rebellion were very evident in Somerset. The cloth industry, which involved many people, was unstable. Inflation and starvation, with the ever-present threat of the plague, made people very opposed to the Crown and the demands made upon them. The county was divided with Wells supporting the King, and Taunton, Bridgwater and Dunster against him. The illegitimate son of Charles II lay claim to the throne, and hoping for great support from the West Country, landed at Lyme Regis. Some 800 men joined him, but most were cloth trade craftsmen and not soldiers. They marched from Taunton to Bridgwater intending to go on to Bristol, but they were pursued by the King's men and camped at Weston Zoyland, intending to surprise the enemy on the moors – where, in fact, they were out-numbered. Many only had scythes or pitchforks, and the number of dead was said to be 700 with 300 taken prisoner.

The days which followed the battle were full of brutal savagery, with hangings without trial, hounding of escaped rebels and public places in Taunton decorated with corpses. Those caught alive faced the merciless Judge Jeffries, and many were hanged and others deported, but some, as the Creech list states, were not taken.

LIST OF INHABITANTS OF THE PARISH INVOLVED IN THE REBELLION

Adams, Robert	Absent, not taken
Allen, Richard	In the rebellion, taken and tried in Taunton, transported for Booth from Taunton to Bridewell via Bristol 24 October on the John to Barbados. Sold to Captain W. Scott.
Andrews, Henry	Absent, not taken
Cornawell, John	Absent, not taken
Exon, Bernard	Absent, not taken
Gill, Nicholas	In the rebellion, and taken to Ilchester jail, tried at Wells, transported to Jamaica for Howard, 25 October.
Harris, Lewis	Took up arms against His Majesty. Tried at Taunton and hanged at Keynsham.
Hearne, John senr	In the rebellion and taken
Hearn, John	In the rebellion and taken
Howse, Nicholas	Absent and not taken. Took arms against His Majesty
Hoyle, Henry	Took up arms against His Majesty
Lane, Benjamin	Absent, not taken
Norman, Thomas	Absent, not taken. Took up arms against His Majesty.
Oateway, Thomas	In arms against His Majesty
Parvuncle, John	Took arms against His Majesty
Payle, John	Absent and not taken
Pine, William	In the rebellion, not taken
Pitcher, John	Absent but not taken
Pole, Simon	In the rebellion and taken
Stephen, William	Late servant to Mr Seagar, absent

Langaller, an ancient settlement mentioned in the Lay Subsidy Rolls in 1327 as Langire, and in a parish survey of 1791 as Long Auler with five farms.

Charlton Manor

Chapter 8
Wills and Inventories

Wills of wealthy land-owners from the 1500s make interesting reading because they mention the family, friends and sometimes servants of the deceased. Besides the bequests to family of property and money, there are instructions as to the burial and service. Money was left for the repair of certain roads and bridges and faithful servants were not forgotten: 'To my servant, a brass pot and a cow for her good services to me.'

The earliest will relating to Creech St Michael is that of George Sydenham, who once owned Charlton, and that is dated 1522. In 1556 John Cuffe bequeathed his body to be buried 'at a Christian burial at the discretion of my executors.' The Cuffes lived at Court Barton, and the splendid tomb of Robert Cuffe, son of John, can be seen in the oldest part of the church. Several wills of Cuffes, Celys and other notable people of the parish are recorded in Somerset Wills, in the Record Office. The last will and testament of Samuel Brewer, in 1764, reads:

Calling to mind the uncertainty of human life and not knowing how long my countinuance in this world, and being of sound and disposing mind and memory and understanding for which I bless God... I give to Betty Cox, spinster, the sum of £12. Also a suit of mourning clothes to value of £3 to be delivered to the said Betty Cox. All else to my brother, Edward Brewer.

The Act of Burial, 1668, read as follows:

No corpse of any person (except those who shall die of the plague), shall be buried in anything whatsoever made or mingled with flax, hemp, silk, hair, gold or silver, or in any stuff or thing other than made of sheeps wool only, or be put in any coffin lined or faced with any other material but sheeps wool.

Heavy penalties could be incurred for disobedience and an affidavit had to be signed in a special church book. Burial in wool bolstered the wool trade and the move clearly had a political rather than a religious basis.

INVENTORIES

The Probate Court required the production of a true and perfect inventory of all the goods and chattels of the deceased before any distribution of his estate was made. This was designed to help the administrators of the will and to protect the next of kin. The time of the year when the inventory was taken gave a picture of the crops and animals in that season. Friends and neighbours made the lists and often undervalued items, but it was a fair way to ensure lawful distribution.

MATTHEW LYNDON'S GOODS (FARMER/BREWER) 1716

Impris money in purse and apparel
Four oxen and two steers
Two cows, a heifer and two calves
One mare, a colt, one two year old colt and one horse
15 hogs, 17 old sheep, 18 lambs
One sow and 5 small pigs and two slips
29 acres of corn
Rood wood and wattle
One wagon, 2 puls, 2 paires of drags, 3 yokes and bows
3 iron ropes, 2 paires horse tackle, 2 saddles, new pad and pillion
Sawn timber and one paire crooks
One vat, one malt mill, one yelling vat, one bottle rack
One iron bar and working toole
Two feather beds and bed sheets and things belonging to the buttery chamber
In the buttery chamber one hanging press, 2 coffers, 2 boxes, 2 trunks
One firepann, 1 pair of tongs, 2 chaires, 1 pair of andirons and one gun
Half a dozen silver spoons, one table bed linnery and table linnery
In the hall chamber, 2 beds and bedsteads, one truckle bed and bed things belong ing and two coffers

*In the kitchen chamber, malt mulch, 200 bushels
of malt, one hogshead, 5 half hogsheads
One quarter barrel, 1 brewing kittle, one funire,
one trendle and bottles in ye buttery
In ye milk house, 1 trendle, 1 vat, 2 tubs, 1 salter,
4 shelves, 1 brass pan
In ye small drink buttery, one half hogshead,
1 little barrel, 2 tubbs
In ye hall, 11 pewter dishes, 2 dozen plates,
1 flaggon, 1 pestle and morter, 2 brass pans,
1 kittle, 2 porridge potts, 1 skillet and one
warming pan
In ye hall, one table board and frame, 1 forme,
6 chaires, 1 Hollandware and pichers
In ye hall, one dresser
In ye kitchen, one table board, one cheese press,
1 tub, 3 pails brakeboard, 1 chair, one settle
In ye kitchen, 4 porridge pots, 2 brass kittles,
3 crooks, 2 spits, 1 gridiron, 1 box and irons,
1 frying pann, 2 paires brandires, 1 paire
billows, one fire pann, 1 paire tongs,
1 fleshpike, 1 basting ladle and one paire andirons
One winnowshed and bags
One chattel lease lying in ye parish of Brumville
one life
Things forgotten and out of mind.*

£323.19s.0d.

An interesting inventory of a lady called Margaret Pyle in 1694 shows that she owned a shop in Creech, and listed are; 'In the shoppe fruit, spices, silk tape and other goods.' These were worth £12.18s. There is no indication as to where the shop might have been, but it is interesting to think she had quite expensive goods to sell 300 years ago.

From 1679 to 1745, 36 inventories were recorded for the Parish of Creech St Michael. The lists gave an insight into the wealth of the person, giving the number of rooms, with details of the contents, furnishings, kitchen equipment, and, if a tradesman, a list of tools of his trade, and in the case of farmers, a list of animals and implements. Inventories of the less wealthy showed how little some people owned.

Books were a rarity, and occasionally items such as looking glasses, pistols or clocks were mentioned, but mostly the goods were practical things for everyday living. Some inventories mention the fact that the deceased owned a shop and listed the contents.

With detailed analysis and much research, it is possible to find which house was referred to in an inventory, but only two in Creech are positively identifiable: those of John Crosse, who lived in Langaller in 1679, and William Godfrey, whose family descendants still lived at Walford 250 years later.

When the inventory makers had completed their lists, there were often odd things left over which were not easily categorised: 'Things forgotten and out of mind', 'Small lumber stuff' or 'Some old things forgotten and not worth particularising'.

George Hooper's animals sounded like a rather sad collection of goods: 'One grey mare', 'one black mare', 'One other black mare and a bay both of Mares very poor and only worth £1.5s. Twelve old sheep and two lambs.' John England's animals seem to have come in pairs: 'Two geese', 'two oxen', 'two cows', 'two heifers', 'two mares', '34 sheep and 6 pigs worth in all £35'. Even the 'dung in the Barton' was an asset in John Woodhouse's list, as also were 30 rood sheaves. Thomas Kitsh in 1720 had a 'paddlestaffe' - a stick for cutting thistles whilst walking in the fields. He also had 'a sow pig and nyne piglets small' and one barren pig, worth in all £3.9s.

The lists of kitchen items in these inventories included a wonderful array of objects: 'ffire panns', 'kittles', 'culendars', pewter basins, skimmers, skillets and ladles, a 'dishcage', a frame of shelves, salt, barrels, 'fleshpikes', pestle and mortars, dripping panns, pot hooks, 'smoathing irons' and cauldrons, 'flitches' of bacon, cheeses, meat in salt, butter and woole (90lbs).

Beds also were interesting items, for each bed was listed with bed clothes: 'A feather bed, one little pello and a paire of blanketts and coverletts and bed goods belonging.' Another inventory listed: 'Tester bedstead, ffeather beds, 3 ffeather bolsters, two ffeather pillows and curtynes, vallons and matt covers and blanket to the bedstead'. John Crosse had seven other beds plus four truckle beds, all with their covers 'thereunto belonging.'

Other furniture commonly listed consisted of 'boards' (tables), 'settles', 'stools', 'candlesticks', 'coffers', 'fformes' and occasionally, 'cupboards'. More unusual items include 'a loombe', 'an hower glass' and 'three Bibles' (all belonging to one person), a 'fowling piece', silver spoons, a clock and table 'linnery.'

John Crosse had many possessions including: silver spoons, bowls and cups, carpets, cushions, a clock and fowling pieces. He had a desk and 'a parcell of books, 90lbs of woole and 72 cheeses plus bonds of £295.' In contrast, the inventory of John Pierce in 1713 lists only:

*Impris his wearing apparel and money in purse
A little old cottage and garden platt
One pottage pott
One kittle and two pewter dishes
An old board and bed and bedclothes
2 old coffers and an old cupboard*

Thos. Ball X his mark
John Chappell

Chapter 9
Ales, Cider and Public Houses

The Danes brought ale to England, and it became an everyday beverage. King Ina of Wessex in 728 stated there should be regulations to govern ale booths or ale stands. By common law a man could set up an alehouse, keep an inn to receive travellers and need no licence. Church houses brewed beer and it could be an important source of revenue. The alehouse would be looked after by the churchwardens, who bought or were given malt. In the alehouses were stored cooking utensils and vessels for brewing. Village celebrations were catered for with parishioners providing food and the church the drink. These occasions were called Church Ales, and Whitsun was the most popular. Sometimes other villages were involved, and on one occasion in Yeovil, the parish vicar became inebriated and was put in the stocks to cool off. His career did not suffer though, as he later became Cardinal Wolsey!

Another event was the beating of the bounds, which involved walking the parish boundary. This was recorded by the churchwardens of Creech, whose accounts show 'cost of processing the village'. It was a time of great drinking. Led by the churchmen, the parish was circumnavigated in procession, stopping to top up at the local inns, but also to hear Bible readings. The New Inn was the Church Alehouse, and remains of the original building can still be seen at the base of the inn within the wall of the churchyard. The inn was a refuge for travellers coming by road or up the river, as accounts show. In early times, the ale booths or houses would be recognised by a pole with a bush attached as a welcome sign to weary travellers. Cider orchards abounded in the parish and Celia Fiennes, in her account of a journey through Somerset in 1689 (she passed through Creech), noted that:

In most parts of Sommersetshire it is very fruitful for orchards. Plenty of apples and peares, but they are not curious in the planting the beste sortes of fruite, which is a greate pity, being so soon produced and such quantities. They are likewise as careless when they make cider. They press all sorts of apples together, else they might have as good as Hertfordshire.

Many small orchards feature on maps of the parish over the last centuries, and on the tithe map of 1839, of the 213 dwellings recorded 190 had an orchard which would consist of only a few trees, but useful to the owner for making cider or for cooking. From a map of Langaller dated 1902, the large number of orchards can clearly be seen, probably unaltered for hundreds of years.

The cider apple trees would be a standard size to allow the grazing of sheep and cattle underneath. At harvest time women and children would collect the fruit using a long pole to knock it down. Sometimes a sheet would be placed under the tree and the apples shaken into it. Two-handled baskets called 'maunds', holding three peck (50-60lbs), would be used to carry the apples. These baskets were probably made by the basket makers in Bull Street. Collecting the ripe fruit could be a cold and damp task, with the added hazard of wasps early in the season. Once gathered up, the fruit would be stored in lofts and outhouses to await the first pressing.

The cider house was often in the centre of the farm, where the process could be carried out after the rest of the farm work was finished.

November 1st was the traditional day in Somerset to begin cider pressing, and this would be quite an occasion and a time for social gatherings of friends and neighbours to help with the work and sample the juice from the first press.

Recalling his teenage years, one villager remembers searching the village for signs of candlelight from barns and sheds, hoping to help with the pressing and then be offered a tasting and join in the fun. The cider stored could be drunk after a few weeks but at this stage would be thin and watery and only offered to tramps and travellers. The later cider was for the farm labourers, and every-day consumption, but the special blends stored in oak casks (preferably rum) for longer periods were for the owners' use on special occasions.

Inventories clearly reveal the importance of cider and beer making. In 1734 George Hooper had 'a brewhouse, and in it were four hogsheads, four half hogsheads, two quart barrels, two little barrels, two firkins and one tubb.' In 1745 John England had 'a

Cider apples awaiting collection in a local orchard, 1 November 1999.

Early morning in the orchard.

Remains of one of the last orchards in the parish near Brickyard Farm, Bull Street.

The autumn's crop is ready for harvest.

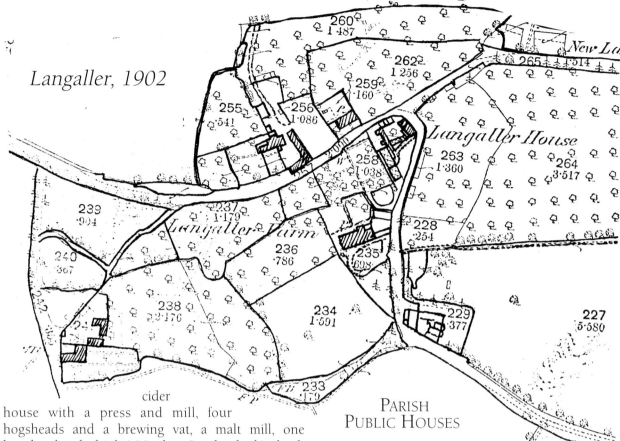

Langaller, 1902

cider house with a press and mill, four hogsheads and a brewing vat, a malt mill, one hogshead and a kittle.' Matthew Lyndon had 'a drink buttery', where he kept barrels, tubbs and hogsheads. He also had 200 bushels of malt, a brewing kittle and bottles on a rack. Will Godfrey, in 1690, seems to have owned a shop in which he had 'appells, cyder and 3 bushels of malt barley.' Jeremiah Newborough had cider worth £3 in his inventory.

In the 19th century, it was customary in Somerset to pay agricultural labourers part of their wages in cider, and at haymaking and harvest times additional cider was provided to help at busy times. Sir Thomas Dyke Acland in a report on agriculture in Somerset stated: 'The liquor refreshes him but wears him out.' By 1887, payment of wages in cider was made illegal, but it was still given to workers many years later, and not until the introduction of more machinery, which made it hazardous, was the tradition ended. In the 1950s, however, when a man came hoeing sugar beet in Charlton, he still expected his cider jar to be filled and kept it at the end of the row - and he hoed very well.

Tom Richards of Creech Heathfield, shop and nursery owner (and bellringer), made cider and in the autumn everyone gathered in the barn to see the first pressing and taste the first juice. Comments would be made on the quality of that season's cider and everyone was an expert. It was an occasion in the village calendar not to be missed. Sadly, few people make their own cider now, but in some parts of Somerset the tradition continues.

PARISH PUBLIC HOUSES

The first record of a place where ale was made and sold to the public was at the Church House (now the Riverside Inn). Here the church made and sold ale to the village, and the money helped towards the upkeep of the church building itself.

In 1582 Robert Cuffe gave Henry Shattock permission for the Church House to sell beer, cider bread and vitals to hold courts, dancing and parish entertainment. In 1630 the puritans banned it. In the late-17th century there were five inns or alehouses in the parish. By 1750 there were but four inns - two disreputable ones in Ham (one being The White Horse).

In 1774 the Ship Inn was joined to the Creech Inn and the area in front of it became a licensed malt house. From 1779-86 a pub called The Blue Ball was recorded and in 1831 there was an alehouse beside the coal wharf on the canal, and The White Lion was at the junction to the Chard canal. This building was still in situ in 1960, but was removed because it was unsafe. In 1851 six inns were recorded, and in 1860 there were eight, including The Star at Adsborough (now The Maypole), The Crown, and, at Walford, a beerhouse, still open in 1914.

The Bell Inn was licensed in 1824, but it is an older building, first mentioned in a document of 1781, when John Dyer paid £500 to William Hussey, lord of the manor, for various lands which included a cottage, garden and orchard. John Dyer gave it to his son, also John, and his widow Sarah sold it to Mary Boyer for £200. Mary Boyer left the orchard opposite to her daughter Ann, wife of Thomas Hooper, with the Bell Inn at a fair rent of £10 a year to Thomas. At the end of the ten years it was to be sold and the money divided between their six children. In 1844 the property passed to John Sloman and William Maxwell Brandar of Stogumber Brewery. In 1897, S.W. Arnold and Son acquired it and amalgamated with Will Hancock to make the brewery Arnold and Hancock, well known in the area for many years. In 1942 the leasehold was enlarged to freehold, and in 1955 Ushers Brewery took it over. Since this time there have been many landlords and landladies, but the public house remains relatively unchanged since early pictures taken of village events outside.

In 1582, Robert Cuffe gave Henry Shattock permission for the Church House to sell beer, cider, bread and vitals to hold courts, dancing and parish entertaining. In 1630, the Puritans banned it.

THE CROWN INN, CREECH HEATHFIELD

There was probably a cottage on this site in the 1700s, but it was a beer house in the 1800s, and in 1912 Mrs Emily Thatcher took the licence and sold beer and cider until 1946. Her son still lives in the village and remembers growing up in the area, helping to move cattle from Charlton on to the moors, running errands from the pub taking cider to customers and going to the village school – quite a long walk every day there and back. But if inns and pubs have enjoyed enduring popularity for centuries, they have not been without uninterested visitors, Puritans apart. In 1897 it was reported that:

A cow being driven by Mr Trott of Creech, from Hankridge Farm, entered the Blackbrook Inn. It went into the bar, surveyed the wines and spirits and seemed disinclined to take any. Someone prodded it with a pole through a window and it left, galloping back to Hankridge Farm.

14th ALE HOUSE

Morning mist winds its way through the trees.

*The Crown Inn was probably a cottage before becoming a licenced house.
In 1912 the mother of F. Thatcher was the licensee.*

*The Bell Inn has been a licensed house since 1824 and has been a central feature for many
children's activities.*

Heathfield Nurseries, once owned by Tom Richards (nurseryman and bellringer).
The cottage adjoining has gone, pulled down as unsafe in the 1970s.

Worthy Cottage, where lemonade was once made.

The Maypole Inn, once called The Star, is on the edge of the parish.
Part of the car park is in the next parish.

Cottage opposite the Northend Mill, where cider was sold out of the window.

The White Horse Inn, Ham, now a residence.

The Crown Inn in 1920 when Emily Thatcher was the licensee.

Haymaking in the early 1900s.

A field of corn stooks in Hyde Lane, 1999 – an unusual sight in the fields today.

Chapter 10
Agriculture

Rising sea levels at the end of the last Ice Age left a waterlogged area with mudflats and salt marshes with fish and wildfowl in plenty. The hunters of those times would have found abundant food around the levels, and we know they lived there because trackways have been discovered in the peat at Shapwick, dated c.1600BC. Later, the land was cleared and sheep and cattle would graze and fish and fowl would be netted. On the higher ground away from the ditches, which flooded whenever the tide came in, people settled – the first Creech inhabitants living on the slight incline above the river, which had an easy crossing point.

Romans came to the area and it is easy to imagine that the river crossing was also used by them. The Romans were skilled at draining land and could see the potential of the excellent soil in the area. Shards of pottery were reputed to be found in the parish, and during the dry summers of the 1960s, field marks near Langaller were seen from aerial photographs. When the Romans abandoned Britain, the land fell into disuse until the Saxon farmers took over the cultivation. They were skilled in the use of the strip system of farming, and by the 12th century this system was well established with strict rules on rotational crops and grazing of animals.

The parish assembly, called the Court Leet, would be held at the Manor House and matters of parish law were discussed, as well as farming practice for the coming season. Many quarrels over rights of grazing, allotted strips and straying animals were recorded. This court remained in Creech until the 1800s, when the old strip system went with the enclosure of land. At the end of Bull Street a few years ago, the remains of a strip field could be discerned by stones marking the areas. (Mr Ron Smith of Brickyard Farm, bought the last strips from Mr Jeanes of Ham in living memory). It was from these strips and the number held by an individual that the custom of wallworks stems.

THE VILLAGE POUND

On a map of 1755, the village pound was situated on the bank of the River Tone, but when the river was straightened, it was put close to a house called Riverside, near the inn. The haywarden (appointed each year by the Vestry) was responsible for the pound, and if animals strayed and were found roaming the parish they were impounded and the owner had to pay to get them out again. There were set fees:

Every horse	2 shillings
Every bullock	2 shillings
Every ass	1 shilling
Every sheep	6 pence
Geese	3 pence

At a Vestry meeting of 1815:

It was agreed to appoint John Southwood to put in the pound all sorts of stock straying about the wastelands and roads in the Parish. If stock breaks out of the field by accident, the owner to pay for driving and pounding.

In 1857 at the Court Leet, the haywarden in charge of the village pound, was directed to 'in no instance charge more fees for impounding stock than is directed and allowed by the Highways Act.'

In the 1300s, cattle roaming the moors were driven into the village and impounded. Some division of the moors was made, but some people were unhappy about their allotment. In one case, a fine cockerel was offered if the division could be moved a little. Records do not tell if the bribe was accepted.

The pound was intact in the 1980s, but the Parish Council declined to take up Somerset County Council's offer to support it, so the owners of the house attached claimed it and have since removed it.

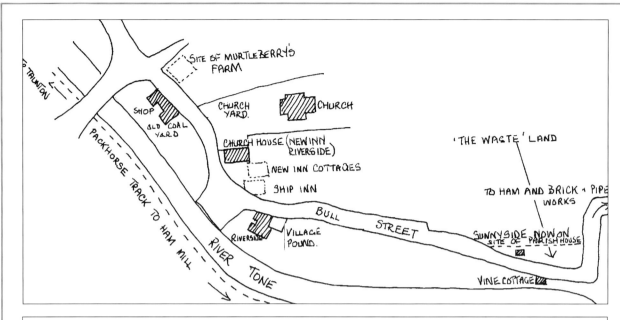

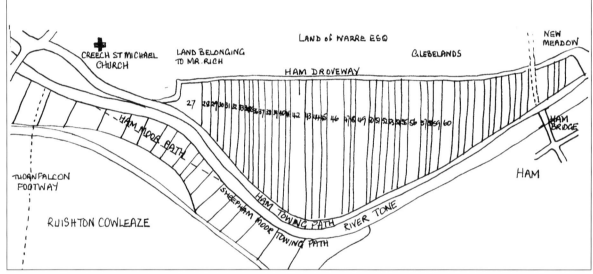

Top: Map of Bull Street showing the site of the pound.

Above: The strip system on Ham and Sheepham Moor, 1830s.

WOMEN

In 1851 Thomas Dyke-Acland, who owned land in Creech, wrote an agricultural report about the area, and included was his comment about women on farms:

Women do all the work. It is true men see the cows milked at a very early hour in the summer and have some trouble with them in the winter, but the real hard labour falls on the women, and very active and industrious they are – but it is a sad sight to see a man standing doing nothing while his wife or daughter is turning [cheese] many times in the day a weight above half a cwt.

Much of the fieldwork was carried out by women, and people in Creech recall the tedium of working on acres of root crops in all weathers.

AGRICULTURE THROUGH THE AGES

As the population increased, so more land was taken into cultivation. The more adventurous peasants went further afield out of the village, clearing and claiming land for themselves and naming the area with field names, many of which are still in use today, including Sharpsland, Bensland, Dibbles, Tooms Acre, Newmead, Hearns Ground, Joshuas Moor.

By the 1700s, the population had increased to six million, and there were many more mouths to feed. Thinking farmers realised that the old strip system of farming was time consuming and wasteful, so gradually, by private arrangement, land was enclosed to make growing crops and rearing animals more efficient. By 1839, these private arrangements were superseded by the Enclosure Act, making the old systems obsolete. The commons and strip fields disappeared, new roads were built and droveways and hedges defined, which made the landscape much as we see it today.

Enclosing land was a complicated procedure and involved several stages:

1. Land surveyed.
2. Ownership and value defined.
3. Land redistribution.
4. New roads and lanes made.
5. Drainage set out.
6. Disputes solved.
7. Finally, new fields established.

A lot of thought and discussion had to go into this change of people's land and rights. Some resented the change and the loss of land or the offer instead of obscure pieces of land a long way from where they lived (which they could ill afford to fence). Many also resented the loss of common land, where for generations they had had the right of pasture, hay and fuel. For some it proved too difficult and they sold out to the wealthier farmer and moved to the towns.

The face of the parish changed as the three largest areas of common land, Creech Heathfield, Langaller Heathfield and Ham Moor were enclosed. The road from Creechwood Terrace to Charlton dates from this time as the hedge on the right hand side indicates. Ancient trackways are bordered by hedges containing many species, which some believe can be dated by a rough estimate of the number of different hedge species every 30 yards, and then taking an average which will give an age in centuries.

In the Charlton Road hedge, there are oak, maple, hawthorn, willow, blackthorn, hazel, elm, elderberry, euonymous and holly, as well as blackberry, honeysuckle and bryony. This was a trackway over the moors to North Curry, probably before the 1300s. In contrast, the hedge from Heathfield

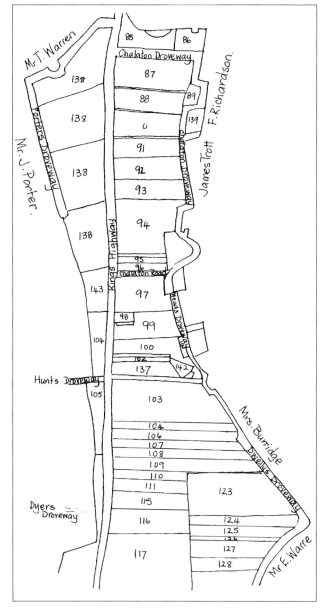

Creech Heathfield from the tithe map, showing the droveways and land portions before the Enclosure Act, 1839.

House to Charlton, contains just privet and hawthorn.

Some of the land in the parish was low lying and drainage was necessary if crops were to be grown. In 1845, Savidge, the brick-maker in Bull Street, recorded making drainage tiles for use in the village.

In the 1750s new kinds of machinery were appearing, and there was more selective breeding of animals. Some of the cattle of Somerset which were referred to in an agricultural report as 'motley and ill-assorted', were replaced by Red Devons and short-horns to give a better all-round animal. Pigs were usually saddlebacks, and flocks of geese were common. These would be kept on the moors for their down and feathers, as well as for eating. The wild fowl on the moors were also a source of food and sport.

*Bathpool Christmas Fatstock Show, 1937. Standing with the prize bullock are Eddie Govier,
Roland Edwards, Douglas Withers, Charlie Bishop, Douglas Hooper, Cuthbert Bishop, Rubin Natton.*

Mr Brooks of Charlton with his cider-drinking pig.

Mr Waites, who worked for Mr Finch, basket maker of Bull Street.

Mr Lock with his baker's cart.

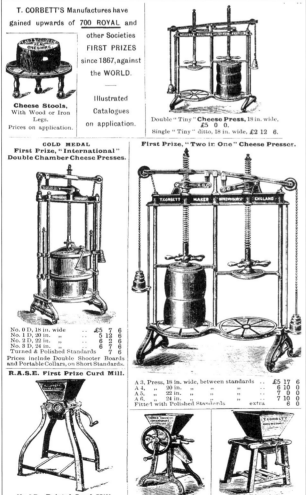

Above: *Old track from Bull Street to Sheepham Moor - note the old orchard on the left.*

Left: An advertisement from the Country Gentleman's Catalogue of 1894.

By Victorian times, most farms in the parish were a mixture of arable and livestock. Most probably had chickens, pigs, geese and some sheep. Every farmer had a horse for ploughing and carrying, and Somerset, always late to take on new ideas, used horse ploughs well into the 1940s. There were of course more innovative farmers, such as Mr Anderson of Henlade who, by the 1770s, was using a drilling machine. The first combine was not seen in Somerset until just after the Second World War.

Cattle grazed on the fertile moorlands in summer, and milk was made into rich butter and cheese and taken into Taunton Market. One farmer in Charlton, who went regularly to the market with dairy products, called into the pub on the way home and over-imbibed. His horse was seen most Saturdays trotting home without seemingly having a driver, who was asleep in the back.

Taunton Market was known particularly for its chickens, corn and cattle (Highbridge, Wells and Cheddar being the cheese markets). Cheese making was highly esteemed in the area of Creech, as inventories often included cheese-making equipment and listed the dairy and buttery as important rooms.

FLAX

This was grown in Creech and was used for making cloth and oil. The stems were beaten and soaked for easy removal of the strands of fibre which were then sent to Taunton for the making of shirts, sheet smocks, shrouds and sails for ships. The sails of the ships at Trafalgar were made in Somerset.

Sown in spring, the crops flowered in June and were harvested in July. The whole plant was pulled and then attached to a 3ft pole and the seeds removed by combing with a rippler. They were then soaked in water, and straw or sods of earth were laid on top, which enabled the stems to ferment, which in turn separated the fibres from the core. After two weeks they were dried and sent to the sutching mills. The seeds were made into oil and the remains fed to cattle.

High labour costs caused the industry to die out in the 1900s, but during the two wars the industry was revived, and today in Creech fields of blue flax can be seen once again.

TEASELS

Also grown in the parish were teasels. In 1189, Richard II introduced Fullers teasels, which were an improvement on the wild ones grown in the countryside. It was a difficult crop to harvest, but the rewards were good. Sown traditionally on Lady Day, the flower heads were the important feature, and when harvested, the cutter needed stout gloves and a sharp curved knife, which was attached to his wrist by a cord. The king teasel head was the first cut, then the second and lastly the small heads. The handful of heads was attached to a pole, about 10 feet long, and propped on a wooden frame and left to dry. Wet weather, of course, soon ruined a harvest, which took approximately five weeks.

The teasels were used in the cloth industry, and were mounted on a revolving drum and passed over a cloth to raise the nap. Their efficiency has never been surpassed to date, and they are still used in some parts of the industry. Many people in the village recall seeing the drying sheds near the canal, and some recall being involved in the cutting, which they remember as a very hard job, requiring quite a bit of strength.

FARM WORKERS

Most parishioners either worked on a farm, were farmers or worked in allied trades. This gave everyone a common aim, and village life revolved around the seasons and the weather. Farm labourers feared long spells of wet weather as they were unable to work and were therefore unpaid. Prolonged damp weather, common in the area, affected the cob-walled houses they lived in, which were small and pokey.

Children were set to work on the land at an early age collecting stones, picking potatoes or withies, bird scaring and helping with the harvest. The school logbooks show absentees when harvesting and withy gathering began. There were many jobs to do on a farm, some skilled and some routine, but everyone worked long hours, especially at harvest time.

The farmer would provide milk and potatoes for his labourers, and with the vegetables grown in the garden, wild fruits from the hedgerows and the occasional meat, people could keep themselves fed, except for during the harshest of winters.

A worry for many farm labourers and their families was the fear that if times were hard they would end up in the workhouse, for if people became sick or infirm and unable to fend for themselves or their families, they would be transferred to the workhouse in Taunton. There life would be made very uncomfortable to discourage people from staying. Everyone dreaded the thought of ending their days in such a place. The school logbooks record a family being transferred from Creech to the workhouse 'on account of being unable to look after themselves'. Many villagers joined the Friendly Society, paying small sums of money each week to receive help in return should they become sick or bereaved. In Creech, The Ancient Order of Shepherds was the Friendly Society to help the less fortunate.

However, life was not all work. Although the harvest was a time of great activity, it was also a time to rejoice when 'all was safely gathered in', and the harvest supper was prepared. This was followed by singing and dancing.

In this year 2000, very few farms exist in the parish, and those that remain are specialist ones with crops or animals, and all the allied craftsmen of the 1900s, who knew the art of laying a hedge, ploughing a straight furrow with a team of horses or forming that special piece of metal, are almost gone – although the land they cared for in the past is still there for us to appreciate.

Theats Farm, owned by the miller family. Mr Miller still lives in the farmhouse and has sheep.

Thatching a cottage in Charlton Road

ALLIED TRADES

When the population grew, roundsmen would come to the door with milk or bread or other goods. The Sweeting family had a milk round and a cart with churns of milk and a ladle for filling the customers' jugs. Mr Mitchell, with his covered cart, brought fresh bread to the door. Flour could be bought at Northend Mill, with beer being sold in the house opposite. The place was unlicensed, and Beaulah Hurford recalled customers going to the mill and coming to her house where she sold the beer by leaning out of the window to serve them, thereby not breaking the law.

The Smithy was next to The Bell Inn, and this was very much the centre of the village, as the smith was vital to the farmer as he needed his horse shod, he required branding irons for his cattle and various implements repaired. William Stevens, whose family lived in the parish for hundreds of years, was a well-known figure at the smithy with his big leather apron and glowing fire. The place was always busy, and William also extracted teeth with his big metal pincers. The sufferer sometimes went into The Bell Inn first for courage, but usually after the event to recover, so one villager remembered. Many carpenters were recorded in directories of the parish in the early 1900s. Again, these craftsmen were essential to farm and village life. The shoemaker and mender were also a vital service for the farm worker, as a good waterproof pair of boots was essential. The miller, the maltster, brewer, saddler and basket maker were similarly dependant on agriculture.

Most villagers kept a pig which would be fed on household scraps and was a prize possession. One local farmer said:

... folks asked after the pig before they asked after the family, and when the time came for slaughtering the animal and the butcher arrived, everyone took an interest.

The joints would be hung over the fire to dry for use in the winter months and several of the larger houses in the parish still have the remains of a smoke house or oven at the side of the fireplace.

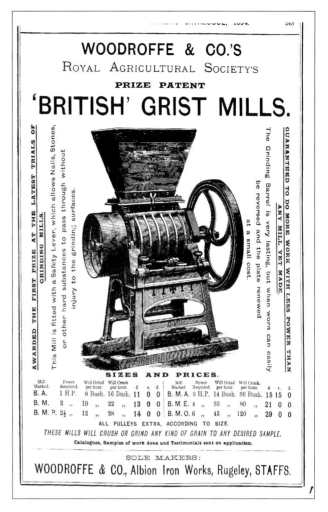

CREECH ST MICHAEL AGRICULTURE SOCIETY (CHEDDON, RUISHTON & WEST MONKTON)

For the encouragement and promotion of industry, good conduct and skilled labour among the agricultural labourers and domestic servants in the above parishes

President Mr H. Sommerville.

The events included ploughing matches, sheep shearing and shepherding, and in later years, cottage garden competitions.

In 1827 there was the annual ploughing match when a premium was paid of one guinea to John Roost, labourer, for having bought up the largest family without any parochial assistance. In 1876 there was a prize given for ploughing. The President, when giving out prizes, said:

This is a time of great difficulty between masters and servants, but on such occasions as these, it is the most pleasing part of my duty to be able to say the masters I see before me, have the interest of their servants at heart, not only their temporal welfare, but their moral..

Ploughing at Creech with a team beautifully decked out in their brasses.

Sheep dipping in the 1920s. The canal was also used for this purpose.

Regulations and Restrictions

FOR

GOVERNING THE COMPETITION.

———•:———

ALL Competitors for any of the foregoing Prizes, except in Class 13, must be workmen or servants of Subscribers of not less than 10s., and subject to all rules and regulations laid down by the Committee. No Competitors (except in Classes 4, 5, 14, and 15) will be allowed to take the same or a less Prize than they have previously taken.

COMPETITORS FOR PLOUGHING.—The name of the Plough-man, and the name of the master or mistress recommending him, and the class in which he intends to compete, must be sent to the Secretary four clear days before the day of competition. Ploughmen must be in the field with their teams ready to start at 9 o'clock in the morning.

The Agricultural Labourer, for working the longest time on the farm or farms, must send to the Secretary, on or before the 16th of October, a certificate from his master or mistress, stating his name, and the master's or mistress's name, the name of the farm or farms he has been employed upon, and the exact time the employment has been.

The Female Indoor Servant competing for length of servitude, &c., must send to the Secretary, on or before the 16th of October, a certificate from her master or mistress, stating her name, and her master's or mistress's name, the capacity in which she has been employed, and the exact time she has been in the service.

Members intending their Shepherds to compete for rearing lambs, must apply to the Secretary for a form of certificate, which must be filled up and returned to him on or before the 10th of May. No member allowed to enter in both classes without an additional subscription of 10s., and then not with the same Shepherd, or in the same parish.

Competitors in Classes 6 and 7 must have previously shorn sheep for hire for a subscriber, who will then be entitled to recommend them to compete; which must be sent to the Secretary three clear days before the day of competition.

THE FOLLOWING PRIZES ARE OFFERED

FOR COMPETITION.

———•:———

CLASS 1.

To the Manager of the Plough drawn by three horses, with a driver under 15 years of age, who shall best plough half-an-acre of land in a given time.

	£	s	d
1st Prize ...	2	0	0
2nd ditto ...	1	0	0
3rd ditto ...	0	10	0

CLASS 2.

To the Manager of the Plough drawn by two horses, driven by himself, in double harness, with reins, who shall best plough half-an-acre of land in a given time.

1st Prize ...	2	0	0
2nd ditto ...	1	0	0
3rd ditto ...	0	10	0

In Classes 1 and 2, four Competitors must start in each Class, or the 3rd Prize will be withheld.

CLASS 3.

To the Boy under 18 years of age who shall best plough half an acre of land in a given time, with two or three horses, the driver, if one, to be under 15 years of age.

1st Prize ...	1	0	0
2nd ditto ...	0	10	0

The Boys driving the winning teams to receive 2s. 6d. each.

CLASS 4.

To the Shepherd who shall rear until the 10th April (unless disposed of previously for One Pound and upwards) the greatest number of lambs in proportion to the number of ewes put with the ram from a flock of not less than 40 ewes, being Devon or Cross-bred

1st Prize ...	1	10	0
2nd ditto ...	0	15	0

CLASS 5.

To the Shepherd who shall rear until the 10th of April (unless disposed of previously for One Pound and upwards) the greatest number of lambs in proportion to the number of ewes put with the ram from a flock of not less than 40 ewes, not being Devon or Cross-bred

	£	s	d
1st Prize ...	1	10	0
2nd ditto ...	0	15	0

CLASS 6.

To the Man who shall best shear three sheep in a given time.

1st Prize ...	2	0	0
2nd ditto ...	1	0	0
3rd ditto ...	0	10	0

CLASS 7.

To the Boy under 20 years of age who shall best shear three sheep in a given time.

1st Prize ...	1	0	0
2nd ditto ...	0	10	0
3rd ditto ...	0	7	6

CLASS 8.

To the Competitor in Class 6 who shall best tie the wool of his three sheep.

1st Prize ...	0	5	0
2nd ditto ...	0	2	6

CLASS 9.

To the Agricultural Labourer, of good character, who has worked, and shall be still working up to the time of awarding the prizes, the longest time consecutively on any farm or farms occupied by a Subscriber 1 10 0

CLASS 10.

To the Agricultural Labourer, under 21 years of age, of good character, who has worked, and shall be still working up to the time of awarding the prizes, the longest time consecutively on any farm or farms occupied by a Subscriber; the time to be not less than 2 years 1 0 0

CLASS 11.

To the Indoor Female Servant, of good character, who has lived, and is still living up to the time of awarding the prizes, the longest time consecutively with the same master or mistress, the time of service not being less than 2 years.   1 0 0

6

CLASS 12.

A Special Prize, offered by Mrs. MEADE KING, to the Indoor Female Servant, not exceeding 21 years of age, who shall have lived the longest time in one family .. ...   £ s d
                                                                                                                1 1 0

CLASS 13.

To the Agricultural Labourer, resident in either of the four Parishes, who shall keep his cottage and garden in the cleanest and best order.

1st Prize ...	1	10	0
2nd ditto ...	1	0	0
3rd ditto ...	0	10	0
4th ditto ...	0	5	0

CLASS 14.

A Special Prize, offered by Mr. JOHN WHITE, Job Master, &c., Taunton, to the Carter who shall produce in the field on the day of ploughing, the best groomed horses, and harness, kept in the best condition, both being the property of his employer 0 10 6

CLASS 15.

A Special Prize, of a Whip, offered by Mr. JENNINGS, Saddler, of Taunton, to the Carter who shall produce in the field on the day of ploughing, his horses, and harness, the same being the property of his employer, in the neatest and best condition, regardless of the value of either.

Creech St Michael Agricultural Show Schedule, 1890.

Haymaking in the village at Adsborough - note the cider jar.

Chapter 11
Creech St Michael Primary School

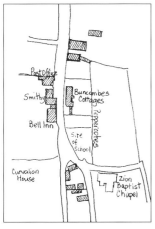

Map showing the school site, 1870.

When the Education Act of 1870 stated that schools must be provided where none existed, the parish decided to form a board to look at possible sites. It was lucky that a site was given 'freely, voluntarily and without valuable consideration', by persons not of the parish: James and Sarah Burge of North Petherton, William Lea Foster of Taunton and Mary Dereham of Bristol. They were joint owners of a piece of land called Peppercotes, which had a separate orchard known as Buncombes, where the proposed school was to be built. The School deed stated that the premises should:

... forever hereafter... be used as a school for the education of children and adults, or of children only of the labouring, manufacturing and poorer classes in the parish... the school always to be in union with and conducted accordingly to the principles and in the furtherance of the ends and designs of the National Society for Promoting the Education of the Poor in the Principles of the Established Church.

In 1887, the school was referred to as a National School, but in 1950 it became a Voluntary Controlled School. It is now known as Creech St Michael Church of England Primary School.

The committee of George Combes of Charlton, Mr J. Dunning, Mr Musgrave, Mr Nicholls and Richard Meade Esq., JP of West Monkton, with two overseers, Thomas Hunt and John Richards, found a suitable site, and an architect, J. Houghton Spencer, was appointed. Little is known about the actual administration or timetable, as in 1890 a number of parish papers were destroyed 'on the grounds of their age'.

THE VILLAGE SCHOOL

Charles Masai, the first headmaster, and his wife, were engaged to work as master and sewing mistress in 1873 on condition of receiving £35 per annum, paid quarterly. This, together with two thirds of the government grant and the whole of the school pence in addition to the use of the schoolhouse, was to be their wages in the first year. Later, Charles Masai resigned as the governors expressed dissatisfaction after an inspector's report (he also kept fowls in the school house garden, against the rules), and in 1877, Edward Tucker took over.

In 1873, when the school opened, the day began at 9 o'clock. Punctuality was considered a Victorian virtue, so the ringing of the school bell was very important. The niche where the bell hung can still be seen on the side of the old building.

Lessons went on until 12 o'clock, when the children would go home. Some had a long walk and others had to include a journey to the mill or field with food for their father or brother. They returned at 2p.m. At school the boys played in the front playground, and the girls at the back. Toilets were two seaters, ideal for gossiping, and were situated in a draughty old shed, which did not encourage long visits in winter. Within the classroom, the children sat on benches watched over by a teacher and maybe a pupil teacher and monitors. Galleries were erected to allow more children to see the teacher, and in 1894 it is recorded that: 'Desks [were] filled for the infants in the gallery'. They were removed in 1910.

Discipline was maintained with the help of iron-framed desks from which the children were unable to move far. They were taught by the 'chalk and talk' method. Any breach of discipline was recorded and suitable punishment meted out, which included caning, writing lines or having to stand for several hours with a slate on which the misdemeanour was described for all to see.

In 1901 a boy was expelled for blacking another boy's eye. Some children were punished for 'insulting the servants of two ladies', 'stealing apples on the way to school' and 'writing an indecent letter'. Later, lunchtime improved for the pupils as they could bring food and eat it in a shed outside the school. Ashes covered the floor, and woe betide those who dropped their bread and dripping! In 1898, asphalt was put down together with some seating, but the shed was open on one side and on very cold days 'the head's wife would provide cocoa'.

It became compulsory for schools to keep a logbook, 'strongly bound and certainly not less than 500 ruled pages.' Entries were made of arrivals and departures, discipline, illnesses, events and condition of premises, but no opinions were to be expressed. This record was to be inspected annually by Her Majesty's Inspectors, and a report on the school given. These annual visits caused much concern and fear in teachers and children alike, as the inspectors would test the children in 'the three R's', as well as also looking at behaviour and school attendance. Upon this report depended the grant for the school and its reputation.

The school logbooks show that on the first day the school opened, the headmaster, Charles Masai, admitted 18 children at 4d. a week. More would have attended but were picking up stones to lay the foundations of the new paper mill. Children of the parish were also busy harvesting potatoes, apples, corn and mangel wurzels in those first few months of school. The head remarked that 'some were otter hunting and withy stripping.' In 1877 Edward Tucker became the headmaster and wrote in the logbook 'have suspended Perrins from school until mother retracts the words she used to me.' Also, the first mention of an attendance officer is entered. In 1882 the severe

flooding was recorded as being the reason for so many absent children: 'Very heavy flooding in the lower part of the village. The roads are flooded to a depth of 3 to 4 feet. Quite impossible to children and even horses.' In 1883 Frederick Bartlett became head and the tone of the logbook entries show his determination to maintain firm discipline – 'no slovenly habits and no fighting' (which seemed commonplace). Children were caned for disobedience and kept in after school and the attendance officer was often called in. A time of the commencement of school was firmly stated, and lateness was not tolerated.

By 1889 there were 142 children on roll and the school was overcrowded. In 1880 the logbook reads:

Harvest is late and weather being exceedingly fine and the gleaning rather more profitable than most years, so attendance was poor until August 30th (from 23rd).

In 1893 the yard was gravelled and in the following year a man was hired to cut the hedge around the school boundary. The school roof leaked in 1895, and despite repairs still leaked months later. In 1897 a number of cases of scarlet fever caused instructions to be given that school floors, desks and slates were to be washed with disinfectant.

Children took part in the dedication of the Diamond Jubilee clock in the church tower the following year and in 1899 a lamp was erected over the school gate. A sad tale of three children sent to the workhouse 'as their mother was not fit to look after them' appears in the logbook at about this time.

In 1900 the school had a holiday to celebrate the capture of Pretoria and in 1901 impurities were found in the well water and diphtheria reported: 'The WCs were to be emptied every day and ashes from the fires placed therein'. The ashes were from big iron stoves, used to heat the classrooms. However, the stoves were inefficient, and when in 1902 temperatures of 40°F were recorded 'the children had to exercise frequently'. In the same year one three-year-old attended school only six times out of a possible 56. In 1905 Mr Hurrell received a purse of gold for his 20 years as head.

In 1908 the drinking water was once again considered unfit, and in this year the first medical inspection took place. Tragedy visited the school in 1909 when a boy who won a scholarship fell in the playground and died of tetanus. Eight days later, when another boy hurt his foot on the way to school, the head was taking no chances and sent the child

Left: The first day of the school's history as recorded in the logbook.

home 'in a wheelbarrow for his parents to attend to his foot'.

The turning of the decade saw great changes for the school. The gallery in the infant room was removed, and a shed was turned into a cloakroom for girls. A piano was purchased and free toothbrushes were given out.

In 1917 a collection of horse chestnuts, weighing 6cwt, was made for munitions purposes, and blackberries were picked for collection by the blackberry man. In 1919 a clock was given to the school, funded by the parish whist drive. It still ticks away in the foyer of the new school. In 1922 the school leaving age was raised to 14 years.

In 1925 S.C.K. Kingdon was appointed as head. He was young and enthusiastic, and for the children school would never be the same again. A visit to the *Gazette* office in Taunton was arranged, as also was a visit to the paper mill. Speakers came into the school to talk about their jobs and experiences, and a football field was purchased. Lessons were taken out of doors (under the trees at Arundells Farm). Village outings to the seaside were organised, and children visited Fry's Chocolate Factory in Bristol. In the same year a note of panic appeared in the logbook: 'The river is rising rapidly as the weather rages'.

In 1932 a girl played truant and ran away to Taunton because 'she had eaten a sweet or maybe a snail from the dung heap', and her mother had threatened her with punishment at school. A teacher cycled into Taunton to look for her.

Dairy classes were started in 1935 and Jubilee celebrations for King George and Queen Mary were planned, with a 'sumptuous tea, sports and a procession... followed by a buffet supper for 1000 people, and a whole week's holiday... '.

In 1938 evacuees arrived from Kensington, Ilford and Bristol. The school had difficulties absorbing them all and in 1941 some 156 children shared just six teachers in only four rooms. In February the first school meals arrived, brought from Langport. In 1958 just the head and one other teacher taught at the school.

Mr Kingdon retired in 1962 after 37 years as head and John Powell was appointed. Overcrowding had become a problem by 1967 and Somerset County Council agreed to build a new school. Records from 1972 show that several children of motorway workers were in and out of school.

The untimely death of John Powell in 1979 caused great sadness in the parish. John Wyatt was then appointed and became the headmaster in 1980 in which post he remained until 1987. Merlyn Brown was acting head until 1990 to be followed by Andrew Brodie who stayed until 1996. Merlyn Brown was acting head once more until 1997 when Michele Godwin was appointed. In the year 2000 the present head is Michael Hawkins.

The original school building, in its lofty position in the centre of the village, is now three dwellings, but its outline has hardly changed, and it is not difficult to imagine the children, boys in the front playground playing 'roundup green' and girls in the back.

An early-morning ritual was the ringing of the school bell, and boys rushed to pull the rope. One morning it fell down while William Hunt was ringing it and the head had to climb a ladder to fix it. In 1901 the syllabus for the year included:

Besides the 3 R's, a recitation of 'Discovering The North Cape' by Longfellow and 'Lady Of The Lake' by Scott. Geography of the British Empire. Practical lessons in basket-making and poultry keeping (chickens kept in schoolhouse garden).

Every child had a slate and a slate pencil. The marks where numerous children sharpened them can still be seen on the corners of the building. Some pens and ink were also used. A report in 1902 stated:

This is a typical country school in capital order with extremely regular attendance and distinctly good work. It is satisfying to note that basket work and poultry keeping are systematically taught in the school.

In the 1906 school logbook we read:

Miss Richmond, pupil teacher, refuses to take needlework as she knows nothing about it. Mrs Hurrell (head's wife), refuses also, as she considers that a person reckoned as qualified, and about to receive a higher salary, should take charge of needlework. Needlework will be stopped until the matter receives atten-tion. I may add Miss Richmond knows nothing about teach-ing, singing or drill.

Mr Hurrell and class, 1884.

The Infant Class, 1883.

Class 2, early 1900s.

The school entrance early 1900s - now bricked up. About 68 children attended here and were of a wide age range as can be seen. Note the bell space high on the wall.

The schoolhouse (1929) which was attached to the old school and was the home of the headmaster. Pictured is Mr Kingdon with his wife in his first year as head of the school.

Jubilee celebrations in the school, 1935. Some 1000 people were catered for on that day in the parish. In the centre of the picture wearing glasses is the schoolmaster Mr Kingdon who organised the festivities.

Class of 1969. Left to right, back row: Tina Watson, Stephanie Bandey, Susan Taylor, Sarah Price, Susy Parker, Nicola Grafton, Susan Watson, Elizabeth Hart, Mark Jones;
3rd row: Sarah Rexworthy, Roy Derham, Timothy Arnold, Graham Bishop, Gail Hopkirk, Jacky Walters, Susan Howe, Paula Huggins, Helen Gean, Jane Lovell, Mandy Plumridge, Debbie Maycock, Fay Whitehead;
3rd row: Nicholas Furlonger, Duncan Small, Clive House, Gordon McDonald, Stephen Bailey, Mrs P. Stephens, Julian Gaile, David Woolnough, Ian Matthews, Rees Morgan, Robert Agg;
front: Wayne Oldham, Vanessa Fishlock, Ann Richards, Angela Tuck, Susan Philpott, Anna Jones, Simon Green, Sally Boyce (American visitor).

Later Mrs Hurrell did take needlework and Miss Richmond did not make the grade.

The problem of erratic attendance at school was solved by the Compulsion Act of 1878, which made parents responsible for ensuring their child went to school. Soon after the Act came into force, the head recorded the first summons, but later lamented the lack of attendance officers to enforce the law.

Farm workers felt that education would not bring in money and although they were not unwilling to send children to school, the comments of one parent shows in what light schooling was generally viewed – it was said by one that if his boy could 'get a day's rook scaring, the few pence he earns from it outweighs the advantages of a day's schooling.'

In 1892 a boy stole a cap and was punished by being made to stand on a form with a slate held in front of him with the word 'thief' written on it.

When the school published its survey of the village in 1971, many people wrote in about their memories of the school. One lady wrote about the early 1900s, when she remembered having her hand rapped with a pair of scissors by Mr Hurrell for pricking her finger during sewing lessons and putting blood on her work. Her brother was punished in singing lessons for not opening his mouth wide enough and had to stand with a ruler between his teeth.

*Awards for swimming, Creech School, 1970. Mr Kingdon, retired headmaster, and John Powell,
the headmaster at that time.*

The launch of the Village Study Booklet in 1970.

Creech St Michael Primary School, not long after it opened in 1970.

The Village Hall was purpose built and is a credit to the people who worked so hard to obtain funding. A new addition of two rooms has been completed, and all of the hall is now well used.

The first "Parish Meeting" under the Local Government Act 1894 — Held this 4th day of December 1894

Meeting called by public notice for 7 P.M. and signed by Wortley Day and William Bolton, Overseers, on the 10th day of Nov 1894 —

At 7.32 P.M. Mr Wortley Day, Senior Overseer opened the meeting, explaining the business to be transacted, and calling upon the Assistant Overseer to read the notice convening the same —

7.35 P.M.

Jas. Emery proposed and S.H. Dunning seconded "That the Rev S Bourne Vicar of the Parish take the Chair" The same being carried without amendment —

7.40 P.M. The Rev Jas. Bourne took the Chair —

7.44 P.M. The Chairman having called for nomination Papers (for Parish Councillors) 7 Papers were handed duly nominated and all declared valid —

8. P.M.

The Chairman having informed the meeting that he would put the names before them alphabetically, for a show of hands in favour of each Candidate — No elector to hold his (or her) hand up more than 6 times, the number of Councillors required —

The names were called with all particulars as per nomination papers, the voting being follows. Day, Wortley, Farmer, 75. Dunning, John, Farmer 52. Gardner, Joseph Arthur, Clerk 50.

Page from the minutes of the first Parish Council meeting in 1894.

Chapter 12
Parish Council

The Local Government Act of 1888 gave powers to the County Council to create parish councils to look at the local affairs of each of area, and to be a voice for the people living there. In October 1894, a parish meeting was called by the Reverend Bownes, Will Bobbett and Worthy Day, overseers, with the intention of suggesting an election day. December of that year saw the first election for the Parish Council in Creech. Those nominated were: Worthy Day, Will Kelland, John Dunning, Robert Howe, James Pendry and James Matthewson. The first meeting was held on 20 December 1895, and John Dunning was elected Chairman. Captain Jenny was appointed Clerk to the Parish Council at a salary of £15 per year.

In 1946 Stanley J. Sweeting was elected chairman and served on the council for 46 years. The Local Government Act stated that meetings should be held free of charge in any suitable room in the school. The Council should receive a grant and no business should be transacted at any meeting unless at least one third of the full members were present, but in no case was a quorum to be less than three persons. The Council was also responsible in this parish for administering local charities.

From a Calendar of Customs, the Parish Clerk had the right to sell Easter cakes, varying in diameter from a quarter dinner plate to a bun, as long as they had no cross on them, as was recorded:

The parish clerk after the Good Friday service, came with a basket covered in a good linen cloth to the Rectory, and gave the largest cake to the vicar. He then went round the village selling the rest. This was said to be a very ancient custom and applied to Lyng, Thurloxton, Spaxton and Crowcombe, as well as to Creech.

In 2000, the Parish Council still meets every month in the Village Hall to discuss parish affairs. The public are allowed to be present, and can speak for an allotted time. In 1999, subjects discussed ranged from the erection of bus shelters, footpaths, street lighting, notice boards, the river bridge (also under discussion in 1676), planning applications, dog-fouling regulations and millennium celebrations. Thus parish issues continue to be aired as was the case in very ancient times at the Court Leets - the subject matter is just rather different.

Parish Council, 1998. Left to right, back: Chris Bevan, Roy Haywood, Stanley (Tacker) Sweeting, Peter Widdicombe, Fred Hunt; front: Gwyneth Bryant, Hazel Prior-Sankey, Norah Carey, Eileen Webb.

FROM MORRIS' DIRECTORY OF SOMERSET AND BRISTOL *(1872)*

CREECH ST. MICHAEL is a village and parish in Taunton union, containing, by the census of 1861, 1121, and in 1871, 1071 inhabitants, and 2304 acres ; in the deanery and archdeaconry of Taunton, diocese of Bath and Wells, hundred of Andersfield, West Somerset ; 3 miles east from Taunton, and 9 south from Bridgwater, on the banks of the river Tone ; the Bristol and Exeter Railway passing through the parish. The vicarage, in the incumbency of the Rev. Francis Samuel Morgan, M.A., is valued at £380 per annum, with residence, and is in the joint patronage of C. Creswell, Esq. and Mrs. Creswell. The church is an ancient edifice, dedicated to St. Michael, consisting of nave, chancel, north aisle, porch, and tower containing five bells and a clock. The Baptists and Wesleyans have places of worship here, and there is a Parochial School for children of both sexes. Edwin Thomas Howard, Esq., Richard K. M. King, Esq., Mr. J. D. Dunning, Mr. Coomb, and Mr. James Bond, are the chief owners of the soil, the first-named gentleman being lord of the manor.

Clergy and Gentry.

Bendall James, Esq.
Dykes Mr. Philip
Jeffrey William, Esq.
Moore Mr. William
Morgan Rev. Francis Samuel, M.A., The Vicarage

Trades and Professions.

Bendall James, surgeon
Bobbett William, farmer, Cathill
Brass William and Robert, masons
Brass George, mason
Brass Thomas, tailor
Brewer John, shopkeeper and coal dealer
Broom William, carpenter, Ham
Buncombe Edwin Abraham, farmer, Theatses
Burroughs George, farmer, Little Creech
Chard John S., cowkeeper, Ham
Coombe George, farmer, Charlton
Culverwell Woodehouse, farmer, Ham
Dare John, "Star" inn
Day Charles, coal merchant, maltster, and corn dealer
Day George, farmer, Long Allen
Drew George, "White Horse" inn, and farmer, Ham
Dunning John D., farmer and landowner, Court Barton
Dyer Charles, boot and shoemaker, Adsborough
Dyer Joseph, farmer
Foster Abraham, farmer
Foster Henry, farmer, Creech Heathfield
Frost Mrs. Harriet, brewer and maltster, Ham
Fry George, mason
Fry William, mason
Gibbs Edward, merchant, Creech mills
Godfrey Francis, farmer, Adsborough
Godfrey Elijah, collector of rates and grocer

Govier Francis P., farmer, Rockett's farm
Handoll John, parish clerk
Hele Eli, carpenter
Hele Levi, farmer
Hitchcock John, shoemaker
Hitchcock Robert, shoemaker, North End
Hopkins William, butcher
House Richard, brickmaker and farmer
Howe Robert, shopkeeper
Hunt George, gardener
Hunt John, farmer, Ham
Hunt Thomas, nurseryman
Hurley George, tailor
Maddock Rosa, shopkeeper
Meade William, farmer
Morris Edward, farmer, Walford farm
Morris Mrs. Elizabeth, farmer, Adsebro
Morris Frederick, farmer
Mountstephens Charles, "Bell" inn
Musgrave Clitsome, farmer, Adsebro
Nicholls John, registrar of births and deaths for North Curry district
Page Mrs. Ann, grocer
Perrin Edwin, farmer
Perris Edward, basketmaker, Ham
Ralls Charles, butcher
Ralls William, butcher
Richards John Simon, farmer, Long Allen
Richards Thomas, miller
Selway Charles, "New Inn"
Sidwich Richard, shopkeeper and shoemaker
Stevens John and Francis, wheelwrights and blacksmiths
Thomas James, shopkeeper
Trott Mrs. Ann, gardener
Thresher George, shopkeeper
Totterdell James, carpenter
Tregillus John, miller, farmer, and general merchant, Creech mills
Trivett Henry and Edward, farmers, Long Allen

Trott Charles, gardener
Tyler Mrs. Caroline, ladies' school
Williams William, butcher

Post Office—George Brass, sub-postmaster. Letters arrive from Taunton, at 7.30

a.m. ; dispatched at 5.15 p.m. ; on Sundays at 11.15 p.m. Taunton is the nearest money order office

Parochial School—Mrs. Grey and Miss Nix, mistresses

Chapter 13
Census

Population census are taken every decade. From 1801 to 1961 the population of Creech was:

Year	Males	Females	Total	Houses
1801	298	332	628	
1811	334	380	714	125
				(4 empty)
1821	405	401	806	
1831	571	545	1116	
1841	660	636	1296	265
				(9 empty)
1851	599	620	1219	253
				(14 empty)
1861	no division of sexes		1121	254
1871	no figures			
1881	no division of sexes		1073	250
1891	496	568	1037	254
1901	518	533	1051	253
				(23 empty)
1911	468	526	994	244
1921	no figures			
1931	469	449	918	265
1941	no figures			
1951	485	509	994	292
1961	495	554	1049	384

In the 1791 Survey of the Parish of Creech in the hundred of Andersfield there were 45 houses near the church and 5 hamlets. They were: Long Auler, Adsborough, Charlton, Creech Heathfield and Ham. At Long Auler there were 5 farms. At Adsborough there were 18 houses and at Charlton 7 houses and 5 farms. At Creech Heathfield there were 15 tenements and at Ham 10 houses. There were 600 inhabitants and 20 freeholders, and Elm was the main wood.

1859, POPULATION 1100

5 farmers	1 baker
1 basket maker	4 blacksmiths
7 boot/shoe makers	1 brewer
6 butchers	6 carpenters
3 coal merchants	3 nurserymen
5 shopkeepers	3 publicans
2 tailors	3 churchmen
3 beer makers	

1906, POPULATION 1051

14 farmers	1 baker
3 beermakers/sellers	1 basket maker
2 blacksmiths	1 boot/shoe maker
2 masons	1 brewer
4 butchers	4 carpenters
1 coal merchant	5 shop keepers
4 publicans	1 miller (female)
1 commercial traveller	1 tax collector
4 churchmen	5 nurserymen
1 coach builder	2 oil dealers
1 wheelwright	1 cycle maker
1 builder	1 constable
4 dairymen	

1931, POPULATION 918

21 farmers	1 basket maker
1 baker	2 beer sellers
1 blacksmith	4 butchers
3 carpenters	1 coal merchant
4 market gardeners	1 mason
4 shopkeepers	4 publicans
1 churchman	1 surgeon
1 petrol station owner	1 bus owner
1 builder	1 paper maker
1 clerk to the parish council	1 surveyor

In 1841 there were 263 houses, 9 uninhabited and one just being built. This is an interesting census as it was taken 14 years after the canal was opened and 3 years after the railway. Comparing this with previous census records, it seems that some navvies from the building of the canal remained, and the trade on the canal brought people to live in the parish. Different names begin to enter parish records for marriages and births. The list of inhabitants reflects the thriving trades within the parish at this time:

14 boatmen	9 excavators
8 dressmakers	6 publicans
4 taylors	3 coal merchants
3 teachers	2 cheese mongers
and some military men.	

FROM MORRIS' DIRECTORY OF SOMERSET AND BRISTOL *(1872)*

CREECH ST. MICHAEL (or Creek St. Michael, so named from the bend which the river takes at this place) is a parish and village on the river Tone, about 3 miles east from Taunton station on the Bristol and Exeter section of the Great Western railway, in the Taunton parliamentary division, hundred of Andersfield. Taunton petty sessional division, union and county court district, rural deanery and archdeaconry of Taunton and diocese of Bath and Wells. The church of St. Michael dates from the 12th century, and is a building of stone, consisting of chancel, nave of four bays, aisles and an embattled western tower on the south side containing 6 bells: there is a curious old tomb to Robert Cuff, of this parish, ob. 1597. and tablets to the Sealey and Trivitt and other families: the stained east window, erected in 1908, is a memorial to the late Rev. James Bownes M.A. vicar of this parish 1872-1901: in a niche over the west door is a singular representation of " The Crucifixion," and on the side of the doorway is a figure of St. Michael: the reading desk of carved oak is dated 1634: the church was restored in 1868, and has 350 sittings: in the churchyard are two yew trees of great age. The register dates from the year 1668. The living is a vicarage, net yearly value about £336, with residence, in the gift of Henry Trengrouse esq. J.P. and held since 1911 by the Rev. John Philip Dalton. Here is a Baptist chapel, erected in 1831, with 144 sittings. Dowlin's charity of £8 5s. yearly is for the poor not receiving parish relief. John Wheadon, who died in 1862, bequeathed £300 to be invested in Consols, the interest arising therefrom to be distributed among the poor of the parish on December 24th annually. Corbet H. H. Cresswell, who died in 1907, left the sum of £400 to be invested at 2½ per cent. the interest to be distributed among the poor of the parish in coal &c. Court Barton, the property of George Coombe esq. is an ancient mansion, now occupied as a farmhouse; the north aisle in the church belongs to the Court Barton estate. There are paper mills here. Mr. Edwin T. Howard is lord of the manor; William Oliver Evelyn Meade-King esq. and George Coombe esq. are the chief landowners. The soil is rich loam; subsoil, gravel, loam and sandstone. The chief crops are wheat and barley, with rich grazing land. The area is 2,270 acres of land and 28 of water; rateable value, £11,178; population in 1911, 994 in the civil and 997 in the ecclesiastical parish.

Creech Heathfield, 1 mile north, and Adsborough, 3 north, are villages in this parish; and the hamlet of Ham, 1 mile south-east, is partly in this parish and partly in North Curry.

Coombe, 2 miles north; Langaller, 1½ miles north-west, and Charlton, 1 mile north-east, are hamlets.

Sexton, Arthur Bertram Finch.

Post, M. O., T. & Telephone Call Office.—William Thos. Francis, sub-postmaster. Letters through Taunton

Wall Letter Boxes.—Heathfield; Church; Langaller; Ham & Adsborough

Public Elementary School (mixed), erected, with master's house, in 1872, for 161 children; William Hurrell, schoolmaster

County Police, Samuel George Jenkins, constable

Parish Council.

Meets quarterly at the Chapel School.

Chairman, William Bobbett.

Walter Fry	James B. Nation
Charles Harvey	Frank Richards
James Mansfield	

Clerk, Richard Jenney

{Marked thus ‡ receive letters thro' Taunton.)

{Marked thus * receive letters thro' West Monkton.)

PRIVATE RESIDENTS.

Alcock George Herbt. Heathfield ho
Biffen Mrs. Castle cottage
Bownes Mrs. Old vicarage
Coombe George, Charlton house
Cox Henry Herbert, Hill house
Dalton Rev.Jn. Philip (vicar),Vicarage
Day David, The Villa
Day Mrs. Bridge house
Dunning Misses, Heathfield villa
Holyday Mrs. Heathfield
House Francis Trivitt, Langaller ho
House Mrs. Linton villa
Jenney Richard, The Lodge
‡Matthew Reginald Wilcox, Adsborough house (postal address, Adsborough house, near Taunton). Telegrams, Thurloxton
Orchard Sidney S. Hill villa
Slessor Miss, Curvalion house
Surridge John, Heathfield
Trott Mrs. Heathfield lodge
Trout Mrs. Hurstone villa
Vaughan Miss, Curvalion house
Wildeblood Capt. Seddon V.D. Langaller

COMMERCIAL.

Alcock George Herbert L.R.C.P. Lond., M.R.C.S.Eng. surgeon & medical officer No. 3 district, public vaccinator & certifying factory surgeon, Taunton union
Anning Eliza (Mrs.), beer retailer, Lane End inn

*Bale William Walter, scripture reader. Adsborough
‡Barrington Robt. Jas. farmer, Ham
Bawdripp George, haulier. Heathfield
Bennett Wm. Geo. farmer, Langaller
Bishop Rose (Mrs.), shopkeeper
Bobbett William, frmr. Cathill farm
Brass William Thomas, baker
Brooks Frederick, market gardener
Brooks George, market gardener
Clarke Michael, dairyman, Heathfield
*Day Alfred, farmer, The Rock, Adsborough
Day David, farmer, The Villa
Day Garnett, farmer, Adsborough
Day George, stone mason, Heathfield
*Day William, Star P.H Adsborough
*Dowell Tom, market gdnr. Adsboro'
Dean Albert Edwin, New inn
Drew William, butcher
Dunn Francis, farmer, Court Barton
‡Finch Arthur Bertram, oil dealer & parish clerk, Ham road
Finch Frederick, basket maker
Foxwell Benjamin, Bell inn
Francis Wm. Thos. grocer, & post off
Fry Emily (Miss), farmer,Dillon's fm
Fry Walter, mason, Heathfield
*Godfrey Wm. farmer, Walford farm
†Hector Thos. White Horse P.H.Ham
Hopkins Charles, butcher
Hunt Hy. market gardnr. Heathfield
Hunt James, farmer, Manor farm
Hunt James Badman, farmer, North End villa
Jenney Richard, assistant overseer, rate & tax collector & clerk to the Parish Council, The Lodge
Kelland Wm. Hy. farmer, Theats fm

Knight Dorcas (Mrs.), farmer, Newton's farm
Leach Oliver, wholesale cider maker, fruit merchant & grower,Heathfield
Miller Henry John, farmer, Charlton
Miller Walter Charles, farmer,Heathfield farm
Mountstephen Charles, carpenter
Nation Jas.Rydon,frmr.Arundells frm
Orchard Sidney S. highway surveyor for rural district ofTaunton,Hill vil
Pendry Arthur, farmer,Langaller frm
Pendry Ernest,nurseryman,Heathfield
Pollard Emma (Miss), shopkeeper
Poole Francis Henry, carpenter
*Porter James, farmer, Adsborough
Richards Frank, farmer
Richards Robert William, farmer, Ham Villa farm
Small Geo. & Sons Ltd. coal merchts
Smith Charles, shopkeeper
Sommerville B. & Co. Limited,paper manufacturers
Stevens William, blacksmith
Stuckey Geo.market gardener,Combe
Sweeting Sidney, dairyman
Thatcher Emily (Mrs.), beer retailer, Heathfield
Totterdell Edward, carpenter
Trott Florence Elizabeth Mary(Miss), costumier
*Waltham William, farmer, Walford Home farm
Way Beadon, builder, Heathfield
Way Rose Hannah (Mrs.), shopkeepr
Webber John, carpenter
‡West George, dairyman, Ham
White Arthur Henry, market gardnr
Willment George, wheelwright
Williams Harry, farmer, Ham road

Others include a bonnet maker, rag collector, surveyor, auctioneer, chandler, maltster, a thatcher, a pig dealer and a silk weaver. It also mentions a printer adding that he had eight children! There was a surgeon called James Dyer, and the accountant to the Canal Company living in the parish. Lastly, John Hills, a pauper, aged 90, had a special mention.

County directories were published at regular intervals and gave information on each parish in an area. The commercial sector gave the trades and an insight into farmers and allied businesses at that time.

Beginning in 1861, the list records wheelwrights, brick-makers, tailors, boot and shoe makers and millers, which by the 1900s have almost disappeared and been replaced by builders, decorators, hauliers, cycle makers and poultry keepers. Some crafts and businesses stayed constant such as publicans, blacksmiths, bakers, shopkeepers, carpenters and butchers. The basket-making Finch family appear in 1861, and by 1931 were still there, as were the Stevenses who were the blacksmiths (still in evidence in the 1950s).

The name Brass, as the baker, was recorded from 1861 until 1931. Less lasting were the quarryman, costumier and oil dealers, although the coachbuilder was recorded for 13 years. Market gardeners flourish from 1914, varying from 4 to 8 holdings over the years, with the name Hunt predominating. Farmers have been fairly constant too, varying from 13 to 22 through the years, many presumably in the same family, with the Days at Adsborough and Long Aller, the Godfreys at Walford and the Hunts at Northend.

Publicans were named with their public houses, though The Creech Inn, or Church House seems, to

have disappeared from some entries. Several beer retailers became publicans, such as at The Lane End Inn at Ham and The Crown at Creech Heathfield.

Creech St. Michael – looking North   1950's.

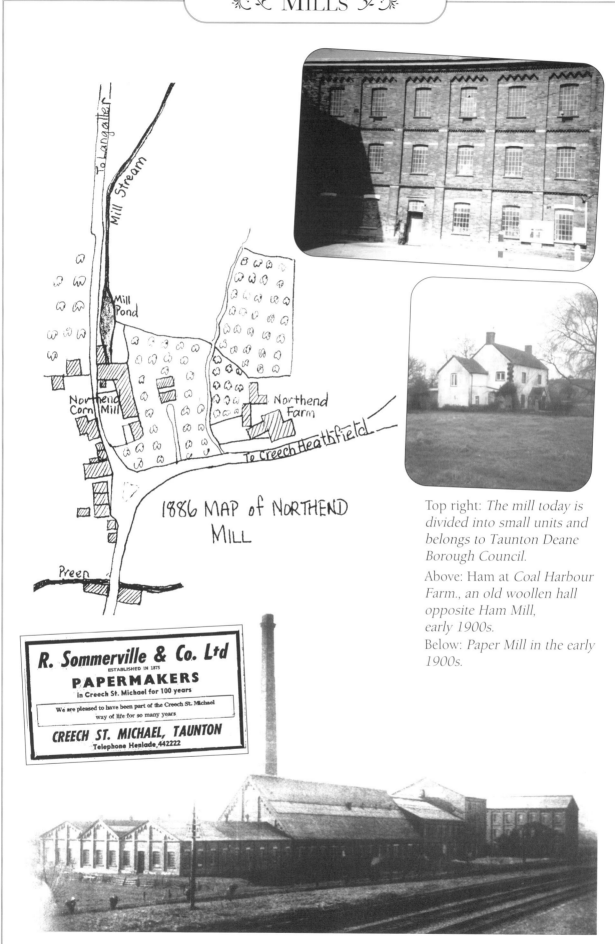

1886 MAP of NORTHEND MILL

R. Sommerville & Co. Ltd
ESTABLISHED IN 1875
PAPERMAKERS
in Creech St. Michael for 100 years

We are pleased to have been part of the Creech St. Michael
way of life for so many years

CREECH ST. MICHAEL, TAUNTON
Telephone Henlade, 442222

Top right: *The mill today is divided into small units and belongs to Taunton Deane Borough Council.*

Above: Ham at *Coal Harbour Farm.*, *an old woollen hall opposite Ham Mill, early 1900s.*

Below: *Paper Mill in the early 1900s.*

Chapter 14
Mills of the Parish

NORTHEND MILL

For many years the mill was disused, but in 1922 George Smith had a carpenter's shop and lived in the miller's house. He also made cider, about 500 hogshead a year (53 gallons in a hogshead). Before this time the mill was owned by Richards, and prior to him Dyer owned it. Water from the original mill wheel came from the Preen, which runs through Northend still.

The mill at Creech St Michael was bought in the early-19th century by the Sommerville family and they planned to turn it into a paper mill. The area was close to the railway and a canal link to Chard. There was a constant supply of water, good transport systems in place and labour available from the parish.

School records of 1874 show that children were absent 'collecting stones for the foundations of the paper mill'. In 1876 the *Taunton Courier* reported that:

Mr Sommerville, the mill owner, entertained the carpenters, masons and labourers, about 80 in number, employed in the building of the new paper mill at a dinner in a tent in the Bell Inn paddock. Messers Sommerville expressed pleasure at meeting the men.

In October of the same year, the new engine and machinery erected at the mill were put into operation with satisfactory results. This trial run was to test the defects before the permanent work began. From this time, the mill produced paper with the pulp coming from Watchet in 20-tonne loads, and the china clay came from Cornwall. Some 8000 tonnes of material moved in and out of the village. In 1946 Purnells of Paulton took over the mill and from this time until 1950 improvements to boilers and stock sheds were made. In 1965 the British Print Corporation bought it.

The mill finally closed in 1983 amid much speculation about take-over bids and its future. The Taunton Deane Borough Council, with the help of COSIRA, made small industrial units of it and that is how it remains in 2000.

The mill was known for the making of fine paper, including writing paper, envelopes, tobacco, art, chrome and enamelled papers. In 1881 it employed 140 men and women. These included labourers, rag cutters, grass sorters, blacksmiths and beaters, washers, firemen, engine drivers and machine boys.

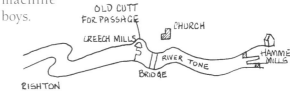

The Sommerville family and mill workers, c.1880, and (top) *map of 1697 to show position of mills in Creech.*

The mill at Northend now converted to a house.

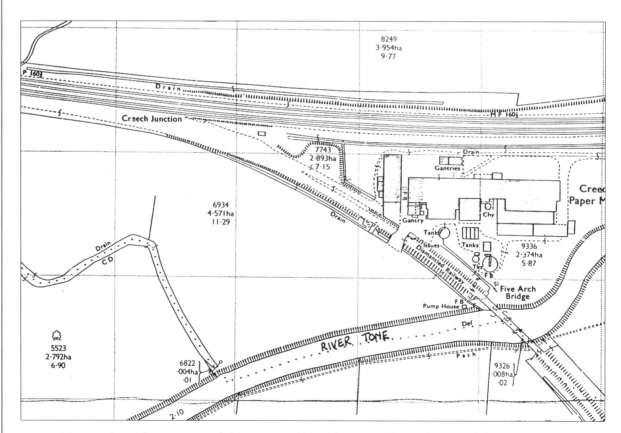

Map to show the position of the paper mill in relation to the railway and the River Tone.

COAL HARBOUR (OR COLD HARBOUR) FARM

The farm situated near the mill at Ham, and near the second cut of the River Tone, is over 300 years old. A date over the fireplace reads 1679, and a coat of arms over the mantelpiece is not unlike those of the Staple Merchants (wool) of London. Towards the end of the reign of Charles I, the River Tone became navigable because of the money and effort put towards it by Mr John Malet of Enmore, and the trade in wool to the Port of Bridgwater began to prosper. Packhorses carried the bales of wool from Taunton along the river to Coal Harbour where they crossed the river at a ford near the house. The house has many fine features including a carved ceiling, half-timbered work in the walls and an oak staircase. On the other side of the river is an old mill and a wharf where the ships came in from Bridgwater with coal and timber. This was a very busy area over the centuries and is mentioned in records concerning tolls, silting and the payment of tithes. Celia Fiennes, in her 17th-century tour of Somerset, saw the packhorses with wool coming from Taunton.

In an article in the *Somerset County Gazette* of 1947, it was suggested that Coal Harbour Farm was a kind of woollen merchant's hall. In later years, an Army execise was carried out there, and a Bailey Bridge was constructed, connecting the house with a secure way to Ham. In the 1970s it was a restaurant called The Cavalier.

Ham Mill from Coal Harbour, 1897, from a painting by H. Frier.
(Courtesy of Somerset County Council)

Coal Harbour Farm and Bailey bridge.

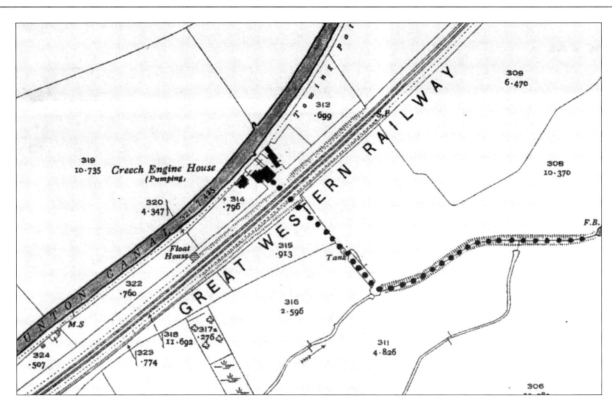

Extract from an Ordnance Survey map of 1889 which shows the proximity of the Charlton Pumping Station at Creech to the River Tone from which water was taken to the canal.

The Pumphouse at Charlton as it stands at the time of writing.
There are plans to change it into a dwelling whilst retaining some of the original features.

Chapter 15
Services and Communications

Creech has seen the following milestones over the last 100 years:

Date	Milestone
1934	First gas supply to the village at Rocketts Cottages.
1957	Upheaval in the village as pipes were laid throughout the area.
1960	More pipes laid to the new estates.
1992	Creech Heathfield gets gas for the first time.

WATER

The water supply was laid in 1933/34, and was adequate until 1964 when pipes were laid from Bathpool along the line of the canal as far as the canal bridge in the main road through the village. In 1968 this was extended to Northend, which caused major disruption to the main road.

SEWERAGE

The Creech/Ham sewerage works were put into operation in 1955, and the village was at the time 'mud and rubble erupting from holes and trenches all the way down the main street' for several months, a state of affairs which warranted coverage in the local paper headed: 'It's chaos, but they look on the bright side.' The weather was very wet at the time too, which greatly hampered construction.

ELECTRICITY

When first brought to the village, many people viewed electricity with a certain degree of mistrust, but as it changed lives throughout the country, people began to accept that it would not 'blow up on 'ee', as was feared by one reluctant Creech user. In 1968, the parish was connected to Hinkley Point Power Station.

Village street with Holly Cottage on the right where Mr Brass the baker lived, and from where many of the village pictures were taken.

The village store, now the Londis shop, 1957.

Village centre in the 1970s. George Sandford is leaning on the wall.
Mrs Floyd is looking at the photographer.

Main Street in snow in the 1960s. Note the garage selling petrol on the left.

Village street when Creech Stores was the Post Office, 1930s.

Rail bridge carrying the line to Chard over the River Tone near the paper mill.
In 1951, the Chard line was closed from 3 February to 7 May due to the country's fuel crisis.

The bridge over the Tone took the railway line into the mill where paper would be loaded and
carried into Taunton and beyond.

TAUNTON PENNY POST

Creech post-mark, issued 1894 when Henry Dykes was the postmaster. Letters arrived at 7a.m. from Taunton via Henlade and were dispatched at 6.30p.m.

In 1826 Bathpool, Ruishton, Durston, Lyng, Charlton and Creech were to have a post once a week. The money was to be found out of General Post revenue, there being no charge to the inhabitants of these places. In 1830 a receiving house for the penny post was to be established at Creech St Michael. The postal stamp was to be No.11 receiving house. In 1859 the sub-postmaster was G. Brass (also the stonemason). Later the Francis family ran the Post Office on the site of the Creech Stores until the 1960s, when it then moved to the Bridge Stores site, then to the first house in Bull Street. Later it was situated in Holly Cottage near the chapel. Lastly, it moved to its present site by the garage opposite the site of the first Post Office.

TELEPHONE

In 1930, an automatic exchange was built at Henlade; it had 100 lines, and in 1948 this was increased to 200. The first person in the village to have a phone was Mr Francis, who ran the Post Office. He shared this line with three other traders in the village and they had 444 as the number with Mr Francis with X1, Mr Brass with X2, Mr Trott with X3 and Mr Bishop with X4. A larger exchange is now in being with STD.

RAILWAYS

The line from Bristol to Exeter was built in four stages, and the second stage from Bridgwater to Taunton was completed in July 1842. The designer was Isambard Kingdom Brunel, known for his engineering skills, which had been applied to the Clifton Suspension Bridge. In 1861, it was proposed to build a branch line to Chard, following the Chard Canal. It was opened in 1866, and a small line to the paper mill was included. This was closed in 1963. The Chard line finally closed then too after 96 years, and the little station at Thornfalcon, which was also a coal yard serving a wide area, was closed, although the yard continued for some while afterwards. Trains to Chard had to cross over all lines to get on to the Chard track, and on busy days this caused many problems for the signalmen. From a book on railways this excerpt mentions the line at Creech:

We cross the River Tone and set off towards Creech Junction. As the paper mill siding appears to the right, the speed drops as the fireman hands over the single line staff to the Creech Junction signalman. We pass the lever signal box and enter the main line and head toward Taunton.

The garden of Creech Station went as far as the road bridge, and was a well-known sight to those travelling by train. In 1938 and '39 the station won a GWR award as the best platform garden. The porters had plenty of time between trains to tend the plants.

In 1960, people would get on the train at Creech Halt to go to the market in Taunton. There was a small waiting room and booking office and 11 trains passed through in a day. In 1928, when the Halt was opened, it cost 4d. single to Taunton. The building remained until the Beeching cuts in 1969. Almost anything would be carried on the trains including prams, bicycles and goods for the market. As the steps were steep from the road, the railway staff were always on hand to help with prams and heavy goods. It was a well-used service.

Reviewing its costs in 1896 the GWR railway company decided to reduce its rates for carrying fresh meat, dead poultry, butter, eggs, fruit and vegetables. Also included in the reduced rates were manure and animal feedstuffs.

People were afraid to ride in trains at first, as they thought that being caught in a tunnel was fatal! At Cogload, near Charlton, there was a signal box built close to the division of lines to Bristol and Westbury. In 1989 the box was taken to a museum by road.

In 1861, an Act was passed enabling the building of a rail link to Chard from Taunton. This was to leave the main line at a junction in Creech. It was opened to passengers in 1866, and a few months later carried freight. The line, after leaving the main track, crossed the River Tone then went across flat ground alongside the old canal line. This land was often flooded. Goods trucks carried coal, minerals, livestock, and churns of milk, as well as general packages. A weekly excursion went from Taunton to Seaton, and for several years the line was busy. Difficulties at the cross-over point from the main line to the Chard line led to several accidents, as trains often crossed over the busy main track from one side to the other. Also, in 1875, a side line to the paper mill added to traffic. The line was closed to passengers in 1962, and to freight in 1964. The mill siding closed in 1966. One of the trains which ran regularly to Chard is now in the Swindon Rail Museum (8750 class 0-6-P T No.4612).

A True State of the Advantage the Publick. by making the River *Tone* Navigable, and a short Answer to the Objections made against the Petition of the Conservators. humbly offered to the Consideration of the Commons of *Great Britain* in Parliament assembled:

THE present Advantages which will accrue to the Publick thereby, besides a future Provision for the Poor by Building one or more Hospital or Hospitals, as by the late Act appears, will be very considerable, by the Trade being brought into many hands, it will prevent Mr. *Bobbet* (who is the principle Obstructor of this Affair) from inhancing the Price of Coals at his Pleasure, which hath been very detrimental to the Publick, especially *Wales*, for Coals, Timber, and Oats; and the North of *Great Britain*, in the Carriage of Wool, and other Commodities, and to the poor Inhabitants of the Towns and Parishes adjacent (who are very numerous and has been the Occasion very often in the Winter-time of grievous Out-rages and Disorders committed by the poorer sort of People, by Cutting, Lopping and Spoiling of Trees, and other ways for Fuel, to the great Prejudice of their neighbouring Gentlemen.

Secondly, By Water-carriage, the Coal and all other Commodities will come much cheaper to all the Country, as in like manner to the Inhabitants in and near *Taunton*, notwithstanding the several Duties laid on Water boarn Coals, the Price being always kept down, since the Conservators did make Part of the River Navigable to above at least 2 s, per Chaldron, and the Queen's Duty thereby will be much increased.

Thirdly, That the Carriage of Tunnage Goods from *Bridgewater* to *Taunton* by Water in Summer time, is not above half the Price of Land-carriage, and in the Winter (by Reason of the Badness of the Ways) scarce practicable, which if prevented by this Navigation; Merchants, Shopkeepers and other Traders in heavy Goods from *Bristol*, *Bridgewater* and other Places (and by carrying back of Timber for Building of Ships aud other Uses) will be very much encouraged, and consequently Trade increased, the High-ways between *Bridgewater* and *Taunton*, being by the Carriage of heavy Goods in Plows and Waggons much damaged and in the Winter-season render'd very troublesome and dangerous (by reason of the low Scituation of that Country) notwithstanding the great Sums that are from time to time laid out by the Inhabitants in the Repairs thereof, which is a great Burthen on them, and by a free Passage by Water, would in a great measure, if not wholly prevented, be of a general Advantage to all Persons.

That whereas it has been objected and industriously spread abroad Coals at *Knapp-bridge* or *Bridges*, and so proportionably for other and Country-places to sign Petitions against making the River *To*, the County of *Devon*, and the principle Inhabitants there and Place *Bridport*, also the Principle Inhabitants of *Welington* and Places imposed upon by the Managers against the said Toll to sign such vigable, all which the Conservators have ready to produce to the same.

that the Conservators desired a Toll of 2 s. per Chaldron for by which untrue Means they prevailed with several Towns re Navigable, for which Reason, the Mayor of *Teverton* in acent, the Bailiffs and Burgesses, the Principle Inhabitants of have severally signed under their Hands, that they were is against the Conservators for making the River *Tone* more navigable House, when and as they shall be pleased to receive the

That the said Conservators do not desire near so great a Toll, but believe that much less than what was alledged, will enable them to finish the Navigation from *Bridgewater* to *Taunton*, and with a most humble Duty leaves that, to this Honourable House.

And whereas the Objectors of this Act, Assert that the River was as well Navigable before, as since the granting of Letters Pattents to Mr. *Mallet*.

Answ. These Assertions are not true, for that Mr. *Mallet*, laid out vast Sums of Mony in purchasing Lands, and cutting through them, in Order for the River to pass through, and by erecting a Lock at *Round-Island*, where the Ruins still remain; and where the Conservators desire to erect another Lock, or half Lock; and will Cleanse, Scoure and Dig deeper, a Place called *Broadshole*, where the Boats and Barges are often hindred for several Days together, and have been forced to Unlade their Coals and Cargo, many times on the Banks of the River, for want Depth of Water, to the great Disadvantage of the Merchants, and other Traders; and will do any other Work, that is Necessary in Order to make the said River Navigable, and that they do not desire that any Aditional Toll, should begin till the said Work is finished.

And whereas they Assert, that they never paid Toll to Mr. *Mallet*, or his Heirs for passing through the said Works, nor for using and trading on the said River, which was granted by Letters Pattent to Mr. *Mallet* and his Heirs.

Answ. This Assertion is not true, for that Mr. *Bobbet* the chief Opposer of this Act, actually confessed before several creditable Persons, that he or his Brothers, had contracted with Mr. *Mallet* or his Heirs, to pay him or them a considerable Sum *per Annum*, for passing through his New works from *Bridgewater*, to that little Place called *Obe-Harbor*, by which it shows that he had no right or property to pass, or trade on the said River, without first agreeing with Mr. *Mallet*, his Heirs or Assignes; and in truth, when Mr. *Bobbet* or his Brothers were sued by the Heirs of Mr. *Mallet*, on the said Contract; he insisted, that the River was not then Navigable, by which Means the Heirs of Mr. *Mallet* did not recover against him, or either of them; so it's easily seen that at that time to serve his turn, he said, that the River was not Navigable, which now he doth Assert for to serve another turn, that it is Navigable.

That the Conservators are ready to Maintain, and doubt but prove to the Satisfaction of this Honourable House, the Truth of all their aforementioned Allegations, and Reasonable of your humble Petitioners in this behalf, and that all the Objections that have been already, or can be made against them his Matter, are either untrue or frivilous and vexatious when and as this Honourable House shall direct.

A paper sent to Parliament by Taunton businessmen, led by John Friend, wanting the River Tone to be made navigable and answering objections to the plans of 1689.

THE RIVER TONE

The Act to make the Tone navigable was many pages long, but one paragraph referred to the duties of the conservators and the work they were required to oversee (1689):

Conservators are empowered to cleanse and keep navigable the said river from Bridgwater to Ham Mills and from thence to Taunton, and for that purpose to dig ye banks of ye said river or other ground, ditch or stream near adjoining, to move all trees or other matter that may be a hindrance to ye passage of boats or other vessels on the said river. Also to cut a new channel, making recompense for ye same to the owners and to cut or open any other stream that be convenient for making the said river navigable... to make a path either or both sides of the said river for watermen, bargemen or other navigating vessels on the said river.

It also stipulates that 'before they meddle with ye land' they consult the owners. A copy of the Act was sent to:

The Chancellor
Lord Stamford
The Bishop of Canterbury
Lord Bridgwater
Lord Godolphin
Lord Herbert
Lord Rochester
Bishop of Chichester

After much exchange of letters, meetings and lobbying of MPs from merchants and traders of Taunton, the Bill was passed, and Edward Clarke MP received the following from John Friend and the conservators:

By the last post we received from the Act of Parliament, for making the Tone navigable to our entire satisfaction. We think ourselves highly obligated to you for your extraordinary diligence, ffaithfulness and ingenuity in preparing and carrying the same through both Houses of Parliament, notwithstanding the great opportunities itt illmet with, and shall always with the utmost ffriendship to our towne and country in general, as well as ourselves, in particular being fully purposed to demonstrate the same in your service as often as we shall have opportunity. May our prayers for your success in the unwearied paines you take for King and Country are the sincere desires of Your most obliged and dutiful servant

JOHN FRIEND AND CONSERVATORS.

In 1490 the Chapter of Wells erected a mill at Ham on the Tone, which was said to cause severe flooding upstream, and to be a hindrance to navigation. In answer to the latter point, the Chapter gave details about the flow of the river:

... all the Somer season the water is so lowe and so many shelpes and bays in the river betwene our mill and Taunton, that it is not possible to convey eny bote that way and in the wynter season, the medewes be so filled and replenysshed with water, that the botes may go over at every place so that they shall not be lett by the myll.

By the Act of Parliament in 1699 the Tone Navigation Act was passed and the authority given for the Conservators to keep the Tone navigable and make tolls to pay for the cost of keeping the channels open. The tolls were set high and traders found it too expensive. Many therefore stopped at Ham and continued the journey with packhorse and wagon.

By 1708, it was proposed to build a half lock before Ham Mill, and that the sand shoal inhibiting passage near Knapp Bridge be removed. Problems for the Conservators continued, as the miller at Ham needed the power of the water to keep the mill wheels turning. Therefore, he held back the water until he needed it, and left very little water for the barges that had to wait hours before being able to continue towards Taunton. The Conservators had to then build a channel to bypass the mill.

The silting of the water courses and weirs, and trouble with the mills, were not the only problems facing the Conservators, as flooding, which happened with great regularity, damaged bridges, weirs and mills which thus needed constant attention. In 1794 the mill at Ham was damaged by floods, and in 1797 the half lock was in a bad state of repair after the floods. By 1822, about 24 boats a day were using the River Tone and recorded at Ham Mill. There were plans at this time to build the canal to connect the sea ports and the hinterland of Somerset by straight and clear routes. This was realised when the phase from Taunton to Bridgwater was completed in 1827. This meant that there were two waterways, and some traders could see the advantages of a quicker route, while others preferred the river. This caused much conflict for the Conservators.

In 1832, the Bridgwater and Taunton Navigation Act allowed the Tone Conservators to sell their ancient rights on the River Tone to the Canal Company and the long-standing disputes between the two ceased.

The tolls at Knapp Bridge in 1699 were as follows:

FREIGHT, CARRIAGE, COAL, AND SALT TRADE, TAUNTON.

Knapp Bridge on the River Tone near Charlton.

Every tunn of goods, ware of merchandize passing up the said river and proportionally for greater or lesser quantity the sum of 2d.

For every weight of coal passing up the said river from Hamm Mills toward the town of Taunton to be paid at the lowermost lock that shall be built on the said river above a house near Hamme Mill commonly called Cold Harbour a further toll of 4sh.

In October 1830 the miller at Creech Mill wanted to renew a mill wheel at a water grist and flour mill. At a court held in Westminster, it was heard that work had involved drawing up the sluice gates for three days, but this had been exceeded to sixteen days, and thereby prevented boats going up the river to the loss of the Tone Conservators. The court judged that both parties had rights on the Tone and should exercise those rights without injury to either party.

Celia Fiennes' account of her 1689 journey to Ham Mills while passing through Somerset notes:

The tyde comes up beyond Bridgwater even within 3 miles of Taunton. Its flowed by the tyde which brings the barges with coale to this place after having passed a large common which on either hand leads a great waye good rich land with ditches and willow trees all for feeding cattle, and here at this little place where the boates unlade the coale, the packhorses come and takes it in sacks and so carrye it to the places all about.

This is the sea coale from Bristole. The horses carry 2 bushell at a tyme, which at the place costs 18d. and when bought from Taunton costs 2 shillings. The roads were full of these carriers going and returning.

In February 1797 John Easton and his brother William were asked to look at Knapp Bridge, which was made of wood and in decay. The bridge was a vital link across the moors to Creech and Ham. They agreed to erect a stone bridge at a cost of £380. It was made of Pibsury stone, with a single arch of Ham stone, and stands still in good condition (*see above*), despite the swirl of flood waters often surrounding it.

At this time, the Mill at Ham was worked by the Bobbetts, Richard and Robert, who leased it from the

Dean and Chapter of Wells. They were dealers in 'sea coales', and owned trows which carried coal from Wales to Bridgwater and from there by lighter to Ham Mill. They also carried grain, flour, cider apples, wool and cloth manufactured in Taunton.

When in 1697 the traders of Taunton wanted to take over the maintenance of the Tone so that they could keep the way open for all-year passage, Robert Bobbett was opposed, as he could see the lucrative trade he had had with boats unloading at Ham Wharf and the business generated from them slipping away.

A shortage of coins in the 17th century meant that many traders had to resort to using their own tokens and they became legal tender. Robert Bobbett of Ham Mill had a trade coin minted, on the obverse side of which is written ROBERT BOBBETT and a spade, and on the reverse IN CREECH 60* RB, and the date 1651/71. This token is in the County Museum in Taunton.

In 1825 the Conservators Byelaws relating to the navigation of the Tone were as follows:

No boat shall traverse any part of the said river without first registering with the toll collector at Knapp.

No boat shall be allowed to pass down through Ham lock on a Sunday after 9 o' clock in the morning and not pass up through the sandlock on any part of the same day.

Every boat, barge or vessel that shall pass up the said river from the said town of Bridgwater, or other part of the said river, or toward the said mill called Ham Mills, shall pay the said Conservators a toll not exceeding the sum of four pence for every weight of coals contained in every such boat,

barge or vessel and the further sum of two pence for every ton of other goods, wares and merchandize contained in every boat, barge or vessel to be paid and received at a certain place on the said river commonly called Knapp Bridge or Bridges. On every boat, barge or vessel that shall pass from the said Ham Mills or other part of the said river or toward the said town of Taunton shall also pay the said Conservators at the first lowermost lock that shall be built or made on the said river above a certain place or house called Coal Harbour, and further toll not exceeding the sum of four shillings for every weight of coals contained in every such boat, barge or vessel.

Two broadsheets published details at the height of the dispute between the Tone Conservators and the

Above: *A photograph of the mill stream taken from the river bank opposite Coal Harbour.*

Left: *Ham Mill in the year 2000.*

Below: *A coin of Robert Bobbett of Ham Mill.*

The weir at Ham. This is the limit of tides in the Tone.

The trackway along the River Tone, used by the pack ponies going from Ham Mill to Taunton.

Bridgwater/Taunton Canal Company. The *Taunton Courier* of Wednesday 3 January 1827 included this report:

The opening of the Bridgwater-Taunton canal, which had been postponed from the 1st inst. On account of the insufficient forwardness of the works, is to take place this Wednesday. The function with the Tone was effected at Firepool Weir near this town yesterday afternoon.

On 10 January we read that:

As we noted in our last publication, the Bridgwater Taunton canal was opened on the 3rd inst. When several boats laden with coal and merchandize were brought up the established wharves on the river, an event which was hailed with satisfaction by a great concourse of people as a forerunner of increasing prosperity to the ancient town of Taunton.

The first boat to enter the canal was the Mary Joyce.

Building the canal was certainly a labour-intensive operation as this advertisement of 19 August 1914 shows:

WANTED IMMEDIATELY, one hundred CANAL DIGGERS on this navigation. Apply Messers WAWMAN and HAUGHTON, the contractors at Bathpool near Taunton.

When the idea of building a canal to link up Taunton to Bridgwater was bought up the merchants of Taunton pleaded a case for retaining the Tone navigation as they feared the cost of transporting goods would rise considerably.

The Tone debt was, in 1803, £13 000, and by 1832 it was £6000 – it was hoped that this would soon be cleared. The making of the canal seemed predjudicial to the tolls of the Tone, and the Canal Company would have to take over the debt, should it come into being.

The passing of the Bill to set up the Bridgwater Taunton canal was bitterly contested by the Tone Conservators, and several law suits were instituted by them against the Canal Company between the passing of the Act in the 51st year of the reign of George III and the second year of William IV, the expenses of which amounted to several thousand pounds. These were paid by the Canal Company. Consequently, the following was noted:

The debt now amounts to a considerable sum, and the Taunton trade being taken away by the opening of the canal the tolls are not much more than sufficient to keep the river in repair, and the debt, including the law suits, on which as well as the old debt of 6% is charged as specified by the Act 10 and 11 of William III, is continually increasing and the TBC company flatter themselves that they can never be compelled to improve the navigation of the River Tone because they have no funds in hand to do so, and that debt can never be paid off.

Another report at that time states that 'nothing could so effectively save the TBC as to convert the Tone below Taunton as well as the Parret into dry ditches.'

In 1846, the Railway Company promoted a Bill to take over the Canal Company, and from then on the Company struggled to maintain its existence. In the 1870s the railway began to neglect the canal and divert traffic to the much faster rail. The Conservators of the canal record many instances of neglect. For example: 'bad state of the waterway and traders in Taunton complain of silting, preventing barges from reaching them.'

In 1907 the last barge made its way along the canal, but for the next 30 years the Conservators made their leisurely annual journey of inspection, throwing coins to children running along the bank to cheer them on. This yearly trip ensured the canal remained open as a waterway and navigable for other boats.

Coal Wharf from the Ordnance Survey map of 1889.

Top and above: *The Conservators' annual trip down the canal just approaching Creech Bridge. Money was thrown to waiting children.*

Below: *Broadsheets published at the height of the dispute between Tone Conservators and the Canal Company.*

The building of the canal was a huge undertaking, and the surveyors' task was to walk the proposed route and plot the bridges and culverts, and any other constructions as well as to look at the geology of the area. The part of Creech most affected was the small but essential way to Foxhole, and the actual main road through the village. The Foxhole way was chosen as the easiest line towards Bridgwater, the main road through Pig Barrel Lane was closed and a new road constructed with a solid brick bridge across the canal.

The navies moved in from Bude and began work. They had only hand tools and barrows, but they managed to move 20 tonnes of earth a day. The canal basin was made watertight by puddling the clay, and the men wore puddling boots. The earth they removed was thrown up to build the banks, and the remainder offered to local land-owners. There was a need to keep the land-owners happy as the canal construction caused farms to be divided, culverts cut and hedges destroyed. Swing bridges were made and cottages built for the canal keepers, and with all the land taken for the project it worked out at about 12 acres for every mile.

In its heyday, the canal served to move goods quicker than by the roads, which were often in a bad state of repair. To finance the building of the waterway, the Canal Company sold shares, with the intention of charging tolls and thereby making enough profit to give shareholders a dividend.

CAUTION.

THE Public are cautioned against believing certain statements which are abroad respecting the effects of the CANAL BILL now before Parliament, whereby the Public are told that they will be at the mercy of the Canal Company, to charge them whatever price they please for Coals. THIS IS UTTERLY FALSE, as the *Canal Company's Powers are limited*, and the very utmost Toll they can levy under their Act, is 2 shillings per Ton. Their present Toll is 1 shilling; so that if they were to do the utmost they are empowered to do by Law, it would only be an increase in price of 1 Shilling per Ton, or not quite *three farthings per hundred* above the present price.

TROOD, Printer, Bookbinder, and Auctioneer, TAUNTON.

5. & 6. Two broadsheets issued at the height of the dispute between the Tone Conservators and the Bridgwater & Taunton Canal Company

TENDER MERCIES,

INTENDED BY THE

Canal Company.

IN answer to a Handbill I have just seen, headed "CAUTION," evidently emanating from the Friends of the Canal, and consequently, the enemies of the People of Taunton, I do assert, that before the Canal Company seized on the Old River, I used to pay *Five Shillings* for every Boat Load of Timber sent from my Wharf at Bathpool; but immediately the River was seized on by the Canal Company, they gradually increased their demands, and ultimately extorted *Ten Shillings* per Boat. God only knows what they would now charge had they not been dispossessed of the River! So much for the Tender Mercies to be expected from the Canal Speculators, who intend to engross to themselves all the Trade of Taunton, and all the benefits to be derived from the River Tone.---Fie on them!!

WM. YATES,
Timber Merchant,
BATHPOOL,

W. TOMS, PRINTER, TAUNTON.

One of the original swingbridges on the Bridgwater to Taunton Canal. (From *The Book of North Newton*)

Vestry minutes of June 1824 included this note:

The said company shall not make the said canal or any part thereof or any trench or watercourse belonging to the same or in across any common highway, public bridleway or footpath until they shall, at their own cost and charges, have made and provided a good and sufficient temporary road, bridleway or footpath for the said parish. Bridges and roads must be kept in sufficient repair by the said company.

Non payment of tolls was quickly dealt with, and in 1857, one George Farrance paid a penalty of £7.2s. for tolls of ash timber. Other penalties were meted out:

For Mr Benjamin Gillets, charge for measuring same. For 3 men at 1s.6d. for removing same from boat. For penalty for false accounting under section 133 of Company Act 10s. a ton.

Sheep were dipped by the main brick bridge in the centre of the village. Industries which grew up alongside the canal were coalmerchants, a brewery near Waterside and a lemonade maker who had bottles marked with his name.

Although in a derelict state, the pumphouse is important because of its association with the canal

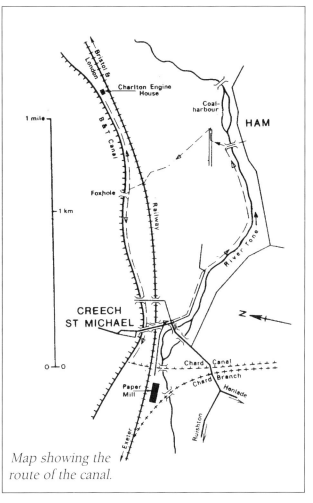

Map showing the route of the canal.

This is one of a number of planet depictions placed along the canal as part of the local space project.

The main bridge over the canal was built to to carry the new road when the canal was constructed

A remaining lock-keeper's cottage on the canal at Maunsel Lock.

Cleaning weed from the canal in modern times – a method slightly more relaxing than using an 'iron shoe'. (From The Book of North Newton)

Youngsters in the village learnt to swim in the canal under the tuition of Mr Kingdon, the village schoolmaster, who used a safe area by the swingbridge to give easy access.

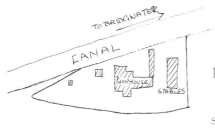

Above: *Blockhouse on the canal bank near Charlton.*

Left: *The iron shoe, used by Sid Hawkins on the canal to collect weed and hay. It lies in a field adjoining the pumphouse at Charlton.*

and railway. In 1905, the building housed a beam pump with a 7ft stroke and a capability of 13 strokes a minute, a low-pressure condensing engine and boilers which were installed in 1871 and 1875. In 1901, two locomotive boilers working on a centrifugal pump, which could deliver 125 000 gallons per hour were installed, but these were removed in the 1960s to the Waterways Museum in Gloucester. Today the building is crumbling, but plans are afoot to change it to a dwelling.

During the war and the invasion scares of 1940, the canal was made into a line of defence with concrete pill boxes and anti-tank obstacles. The swing bridge mechanisms were destroyed also.

In 1947, the canal went into public ownership, and in 1952 the Waterways Company planned recreational activities along its course. In 1960, it came under the management of British Waterways.

Until the late 1960s, the Canal Company employed canal keepers who, with their boats specially designed for the canal, kept down the weed, trimmed the edges and generally kept an eye on the waterway. Sid Hawkins and his sister lived in the

Engine Cottage at Charlton, and he managed the canal several miles either side of the pump house adjoining his cottage. He was a familiar figure and knew every plant, bird and animal which lived by the canal. He kept the water free from weed, which often clogged the flow of water, and was a source of information about canal matters.

Sadly the Canal Company found new ways of keeping the water flowing well, and Sid became redundant. Those who walked the towpath in the 1960s will remember him as part of canal life and mourn the passing of quiet waterways and the way of life he represented.

The 'Rules for Bathing in the Canal' were outlined at the Parish Council Meeting, 11 May 1927. Present were the Chairman, Messrs Foxwell, Harvey, Bright, Mansfield Miller and Richards. The clerk reported having permission from the Ministry of Health re the adoption of Baths and Wash houses Act. The bathing committee

The Pumphouse at Charlton

115

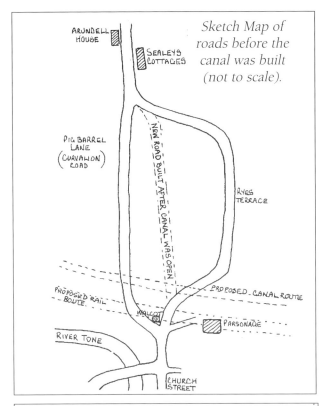

Sketch Map of roads before the canal was built (not to scale).

Looking from bridge toward Taunton these two cottages were on the junction of Chard Canal. One was a public house – The White Lion.

(represented by Messrs Kingdon and Warren), presented their proposed rules and regulations for the conduct of the bathing pool:

The swimming pool is used at the risk of the bather. The Parish Council or Members of the Committee are in no way responsible for any loss or accident.

The bathing hut is for the use of residents in the parish, others than residents will be allowed to bathe on the payement of one penny per bathe, or an annual payment of 1 shilling.

Regulation bathing costumes must be worn, any person infringing this rule will be prosecuted.

The hut and pool will be reserved on certain days for the use of ladies only. Mixed bathing is strictly prohibited under any circumstances.

Any person found damaging the hut, committing any nuisance whatsoever or using bad language, will be liable to prosecution.

The hut will be open at certain specific times, bathing at other than those times is strictly prohibited.

When instruction in swimming, diving or lifesaving is being given, all other bathers must obey instructions of person in charge.

Members of this Parish Council or of the Bathing Committee, have the powers to ban any person from the use of the bathing place, the cause of such is to be reported to the Council.

Bathing on Sundays after 10a.m. is strictly forbidden.

The limits of the bathing pool are from the posts on the south (?). Persons exceeding these limits will be prohibited from using the pool.

... Removal of the life-saving apparatus is strictly forbidden except when required for saving life. Suggested apparatus to be one lifebelt with rope and 2 12ft. poles.

Mr Foxwell proposed these rules be adopted and it was carried unanimously. Mr Harvey presented two estimates for the shed, one from Mr F. Poole at £14 and one from Mr Geo. Smith at £11.0s.10d. It was proposed by Mr Miller and carried that Mr Geo. Smith's estimate be accepted.

Some villagers recollect being given a bar of soap and told to take a bath in the canal. When the canal was constructed, there was a need to build 11 brick bridges and 12 wooden swing bridges to link divided farms (see page 109).

In 1886, the canal was closed for six weeks and 500 to 600 men, under the guidance of Mr Hammet, an engineer from Taunton, began clearing the canal. From the 14 miles of its length, an estimated 130 000 tons of mud and debris was removed, a considerable proportion of which was utilised by occupants of adjacent land. The rest was banked alongside the hedges, thus improving the towing path. By September 1886, water was let in between Taunton and Maunsell Lock, but the rest was not filled until Bridgwater Dock gates were repaired. While this was happening, the Severn Tunnel was completed, making a cheaper route for coal.

One lady remembers as a child sitting on a coil of rope on her father's barge, going to Bridgwater to fetch coal to bring back to Creech. Her mother would sit and knit. They would have a long wait in Bridgwater, so it would be dark on their return. She remembers the quiet and the occasional noise in the water which frightened her. She was always pleased to see the bridge at Creech come into view.

Typical canal barge.

Above: *The remains of the Chard Canal bridge over the Tone near the paper mill.*

Left: *River Authority scientists looking at the state of fish in the canal in 1997 concluded the canal's fish population to be healthy. The fish caught included pike, tench, roach, rudd, gudgeon and bream.*

CHARD CANAL

Map to show the Chard Canal.

In 1830, a group of businessmen agreed to back the building of a canal to link Chard and Ilminster with Taunton. James Green was asked to draw up plans for a canal 13 miles long and only 23 feet wide. It would leave the Taunton Canal at Creech.

In 1834, the Act to authorise the plan was passed, and by 1835 it was in progress. It took four years to complete as it went through hilly country, which necessitated building two tunnels and four inclines. However, the use of tugboats instead of narrowboats meant that there was no need to have locks. In 1841, the canal opened as far as Ilminster, and in 1842, it continued on to Chard:

Notice is hereby given that this canal will be open for traffic from Bridgwater Taunton Canal to Ilminster on Thursday 15th July inst. By order of the committee of management

Issac Cook and Sons, Clerk.

The total cost of building was approximately £57 000 but unfortunately, the railway came to the fore, and the line to Chard was constructed by 1866, thus making the Chard Canal a less favourable way of transporting goods. This amazing feat of engineering was to last only until 1867 when it closed, but the line can be traced from the Bridgwater Taunton Canal close to the paper mill.

Floods at Hopkins Abbatoir and the milk is being delivered by boat, 1922.

Flood in the village, 1910.

FLOODING IN THE PARISH

Since records began the low-lying areas of the parish have flooded, causing disruption to travel and to farming. In 1960, the area suffered severe flooding when homes in Creech and Taunton were damaged by water. When the floods subsided, the River Board engineers started to investigate a flood alleviation programme, and in 1964, the Ministry approved a scheme which would enlarge and widen the Tone from Taunton to its confluence with the River Parret at Burrowbridge.

C.D. Dobbie and Partners were the consultant engineers, and their plan was to deepen and widen the river between 30 and 40 feet (it was a maximum 50 ft wide previously). The scheme meant the removal of several farm buildings and some dwellings, and an extra cut at the river bridge in Creech, where the river narrowed.

A new bridge was built, ditches were widened and reconstructed, and the arches of the old aqueduct opened up to allow freer movement of water.

Since these and other structures have been in place, flooding has been kept to a minimum. Although the moors and area around Creech aqueduct still flood, the huge problems encountered in 1960 have not been repeated.

The farmhouse at Durmans over the canal at Charlton was made of cob and during the 1960 floods it fell down with the occupants inside. Miraculously, they escaped with minor injuries, but the house was demolished and a bungalow built as the farmhouse.

Floods were disastrous for school attendance. In 1874 we read 'an extremely wet day, the waters were up so that children from Ham could not get to school' and 'waters up again today and many children away as a consequence.'

In 1833 the following piece of advice was given to the Overseers of the Moors by the Commissioner of Sewers:

The Overseers were asked to look at drains and walls to see if they were in order. If the offender be humble, fine 2s. If he be recalcitrant he must be threatened with the County Court – better to joke and coax him into confession.

Above: *Postman Hooper cycling through the floods, 1960s.*
Below: *Nora Drewe and Mary Mitchell chatting during the Northend floods, 1961.*

Roller at the beginning of Bull Street, c.1914.

Village street looking towards Northend down Coxs Hill, 1900.

Creech children at work on their traffic survey in 1970.

Children during the 1970 survey measuring across the original village street in Laburnum Terrace.

ROADS

The Upkeep of Roads Act of 1555 decreed that constables and churchwardens of a parish should at Easter Week elect two honest and upright persons to be surveyors and orderers for the year. If not doing the duty they were to be fined 20 shillings. It was further enacted that every parishioner, for each plough and in tillage or pasture that he occupied, and every other person possessing a team or plough, should send a wain or cart with oxen or horses, spades, picks and other necessary tools, in charge of able men to work on the roads under the surveyors' direction for six days a year, servants to be sent by the gentry. This scheme was in operation for 300 years, and the surveyor put in a report to the Justice of Peace. He had to ensure that occupiers of land adjoining the highway kept ditches and drains clear and hedges cut, and also that all obstructions were removed to enable clear passage to vehicles.

This Act was abolished in 1835, and a general highway rate introduced: 'Each foot, horse or cartway must be kept open and covered in sand and gravel.'

Roads in the parish were mainly earth with stones rolled into them, as can be seen in the photograph of the roller at the beginning of Bull Street. Other pictures show the state of the main road through the village. It is little wonder the boot and shoemaker was kept busy. When Harry Frier painted a scene of the main street in 1895 it was just a dirt road. The repairing of roads in Creech and the maintenance of the poor were two problems faced by officials in the parish, so the solution was to let the poor mend the roads.

The Labour on the Highway records are detailed, and from April 1853 to 1854 the cost to the parish was £56.13s.3d. This would include the flint and gravel used. The stones and rubble came from Combe, the flint from Buckland St Mary and Blagdon Hill, and the gravel from the gravel pits at Creech Heathfield. Jobs recorded at this time were:

Breaking of stone
   (7 tonnes)
Breaking of flint
   (2 tonnes)
Spreading 73 tonnes of stone
Carrying rubble
Hauling stone
97 tonnes of scrapings
Raking the road
Yarding

Bills included sums for the carting of stone and the cost of drain tiles, made by Savidge the brick-maker in Bull Street. A carpenter, smith, mason and haulier also had to be paid. The cost of maintaining roads was high in this area where flooding caused so much damage.

Roadmen did a twice-yearly survey to look at the vehicles using the highway. They checked to see if carriages were using the permitted number of horses and to see if the roads were in need of repair. They were also expected to supervise any roadworks in the parish.

When the Creech schoolchildren did their traffic survey in 1970, they counted the number of vehicles passing through the village from 8a.m. to 9a.m. and recorded 315. Lorries were then allowed through the village and therefore counted. With the additional housing in the parish it must have at least trebled the traffic on the road.

An article in the *Taunton Times* recently headlined 'Traffic Dangers Must Be Tackled' expressed the concern of the Parish Council regarding the excess traffic passing through the village, and the parking problems around the shop and Post Office. Despite a series of traffic-calming measures, people still travel too fast and park in dangerous places.

The village is a focus for people to shop in their own locality, and the Post Office attracts many customers, but parking space is limited and at school times there is a huge surge of cars. Parents need to be encouraged to walk the children to school rather than bring the car into Hyde Lane. Better parking facilities are needed if local shops are to survive and help to create a thriving community.

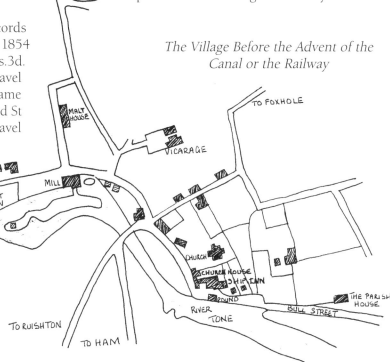

The Village Before the Advent of the Canal or the Railway

BRIDGES

In 1627 a petition from the inhabitants of Creech was made to the magistrates of Taunton as they wanted some support with bridge repairs, for it was:

... not only the timberwork of Creech Bridge which they are bound to repair, but also the arches and piers are becoming very (?) and they are burdened with the repairs of Ham Bridge.

The reply came as follows: 'The Bench will order the bridge to be viewed and ordered that other places help with the charges.' The Bench did indeed order the work to be carried out, but by 1628 nothing had been done. In 1777 we encounter a similar story when the following report was made:

We present the Bridge called New Bridge being out of repair and in much danger of a persons life. It has been a church path time out of mind and ever repaired by the occupier of Coalharbour, which are at present James Stowey and Company, being the present occupier, we present them to put the said bridge in good repair and done by 25th December.

By 1779 nothing had been done, and in 1780 it was still a problem.

HORSE-DRAWN TRANSPORT AND MORE

Mr Francis, who owned a village shop where the Creech Stores now stands, kept a large number of horse-drawn vehicles, including one Brougham, a single-horse brake, a Victoria, a double-horse brake, a landau, two wagonettes and one other vehicle.

He kept ten horses stabled where West View now is. Men in livery drove the vehicles, and one regular job in the 1900s was taking the vicar's wife for an afternoon's drive. He also ran the first horse-drawn bus in the village. Mr Willmott of Northend bought out the wagonette and continued the service at a fare of one shilling return to Taunton – and there was no waiting for a tardy passenger.

Mr Duke of The New Inn had the first motorbike with a basket sidecar.

Mr Mitchell ran the first bus through Creech in 1915. It was a Renault and went from Creech Heathfield through Ruishton to Taunton. The fares were 10d. from Crown Lane, 8d. from Creech Halt and 6d. from Ruishton. When the seats were full the driver called out 'Get the boards out Mother!' and the boards would be placed across from seat to seat to make more room. The service was taken over by Western National in 1946. (Information from Shirley Mitchell in the *Creech Village Study*, 1971.).

Top: *New bridge erected over the canal.*
Second from top: *Main bridge over the Tone taking the road to Ruishton.*
Third from top: *Ham footbridge.*
Bottom: *New bridge over the river cutting built in 1970.*

Village street in the early 1900s.

Snowy Creech from the church tower, 1908.

Tate and Lyle's van, with Tom Dominey working on it in the 1950s. Tate and Lyles are a well-known sugar manufacturers, and they had a depot for the distribution of sugar at Walford Cross. Many parishioners worked there and sugar was delivered to shops from tiny village stores to large town shops. The company closed in 1976 and was bought by Langdons.

One of the first motorbikes seen in the village. Herbie Duke is in the sidecar.

PARISH PATHS

Parish paths were numbered and catalogued with descriptions of the path as to whether it was a footpath or bridleway, and this was recorded on a large parish map held by the Parish Council. For example:

From: county road known as Charlton Road at Myrtle House (now demolished, but was at the entrance to Meads Droveway)

To: Durston Parish boundary.

Description: The path is a footpath. It starts at the County Road known as Charlton Road at Myrtle House, opposite North End of path no.12 and proceeds in a northerly direction along the west side of an orchard (past The Crown Inn), to Theats Farm and junction of path no.14. The path continues *northerly to Parish boundary south south west of Drakes Barton (now H. Bults).*

All the latter half of this path has now disappeared because of the motorway and the building of the new road to Durston Elms.

The footpaths and bridleways were vital links in days gone by, as people walked to and from work and to social events. The doctor's path, linking Durston and Creech, was well used as Durston folk had no doctor, so had to walk to Creech Heathfield where the doctor lived. Before this time everyone had to go to Taunton, as is recorded in the churchwardens' accounts.

Above: *The above path was known as Charlton Droveway and this is the beginning of the path described.*

Right: *The blacksmiths when the Pincombes lived there.*

Below right: *Canal Festival of boats in the 1990s.*

Village Street 1885

Chapter 16
Sports and Parish Activities

Village Outings and Events

Originally the village outing was organised to send children from the parish to the seaside at a time when there was very little chance of them ever seeing the sea for themselves. It began in the 1930s and a train ride was the first outing. Carriages were reserved on the train to either Teignmouth or Weymouth and the people would get on at Creech Halt. Tea was provided at a restaurant for everyone. When the train fare began to become too costly, Osmonds Coaches took the villagers and sometimes there would be up to nine vehicles leaving from under the chestnut tree opposite the school. All of the children would be given half a crown to spend at the seaside, or for a fish-and-chip supper on the way home. The village headmaster, Mr Kingdon, expected his staff to go on the outing, and he treated them to a high tea on the day.

The funds to pay for the outing were raised by the Outing Committee, who organised a twice-yearly event of a whist drive and dance in the WI hall. Local businesses gave prizes for a grand raffle, and the main prize was often a piece of meat or poultry. People were very generous and funds were raised for many years for this event until the committee decided it was no longer needed and in the early 1980s it disbanded.

Another village event was the fête. This was a long-standing occasion as photographs show. Maypole dancing and sports, as well as stalls, were set up, sometimes in the Vicarage grounds and sometimes in a field. Everyone took part and each village association had a stand to raise funds for the church. The school took it on in latter years, but several have been held in the new Vicarage gardens when the town band played and people enjoyed the entertainment provided.

Village outing to Cheddar – at a speed of 12 miles per hour

Maypole dancing was always a feature of village fêtes.

Crowning the School Fête Queen, 1973. Left to right, back: Rachel Westlake, Kay Coles, Tracey Shattock, Karen Villiers, Janet Pugh; middle: Amanda Strutt (kneeling), Louise Bartlett, Claire Leigh, Helen Jenkins; front: Lisa Batstone and Diane Hole (two tiniest ones).

Village fête in the Vicarage grounds, with the mill owner, Mr Sommerville, on the left, and the two Miss Bobbets behind the stall.

Village fête, 1904.

Left: *Tristram Foxwell, born in the village – a national floral display judge and well-known local artist. Photograph, 1950.*

Below: *Village Flower Show, 1998 and Lesley McDowell views the exhibits.*

Bottom right: *Doctor Bowthorpe playing another role at a village show.*

Bottom left: *Mr and Mrs Lawrence enjoying the village fête in the Vicarage grounds.*

SPORTS AND PARISH ACTIVITIES

Silver Jubilee celebrations in the parish cost £77.10s.1d. Meticulous accounts were kept by Mr S. Kingdon (headmaster), and great were the celebrations which included a huge feast. Collections were made throughout the parish and food was given which was listed as including sausages, groceries, meat, beer, milk, butter, bread, cakes and pies. Children's sports took place and 300 children received a celebration mug. There was a band paid for, and the day included a dance and social, where ice cream, cider and lemonade was purchased. One mystery item was '27 invalids at 2s. each'!

For the celebration of the Queen's Diamond Jubilee Mr Frost suggested:

Recreational field for residents,
Tea for the children and a clock in the
    church tower,
Ambulance car for the village
Drinking fountain,
Public cemetery
Lighting in the village

It was suggested that all these things be considered by the council. A correspondent signing himself 'Loyalty', wrote to the paper:

Surely, no parish in Somerset will equal Creech St Michael in generosity or loyalty at the forthcoming Diamond Jubilee celebrations when, after five meetings to consider the advisability of putting a clock into the parish church, it was found that from roughly 1000 inhabitants only £63 could be raised whilst the clock costs £85. It was finally decided to do nothing. God save the Queen.

Sports have always been an important part of village life – among them cricket and football teams, tug-of-war, children's sports and skittles. In later years, a playing field was made, and sport had its own parish venue.

Previous to this, a football and cricket pitch existed on a field at Creech Heathfield, opposite the doctor's. There were often complaints about bad language on the pitch. The village football team thrived in the 1960s and won the league one year. The cricket team, meanwhile, played regularly. In the early 1900s, the mill had a good tug-of-war team, who beat all comers, and from the photographs looked formidable.

At all of the fêtes a skittles match for a pig would take place. Both men and women took part and the match was set up in the Bell paddock and went on all day. Skittles has always been a tradition in the area, and most pubs had a team, as many still do.

As part of the Whitsun festivities in the parish many years ago there were the races which were considered to be very important. Many people still remember winning and receiving a coin as a prize.

Madge Stace opening the new recreation ground in Hyde Lane.

Celebrations outside the New Inn for the Coronation of King George V, 1910.

The paper mill tug-of-war team, 1906.

Creech Rovers Football Club, 1913/14.

Creech Football Team, 1957. Left to right, back row: Eric Price, George Sweeting, Bernard Priddle, Bert Lee, John Holley, Jim Forsyth, ? Woodman, Les Poster, Fred Vile – with crutches (Chilly Vile); front: ?, Eric Finlayson, Les James.

An unnamed parish athlete obviously well pleased with himself.

Village Football Team, 1960. Left to right, back: George Bartlett, Fred Ketch, John Counsell, Tony Foyle, Robin Small; front: Ken Widger, Ron Wadham, Bernard Priddle, John Holley, Chris Ellett.

Creech British Legion Skittles Team, pictured in their home alley at the Bell Inn, 1950. Left to right, back: Jack Storey, Tris Foxwell, Jack Holley, Owen Hutchins, Brian Foxwell; middle: Digger Wyatt, Ted Coleman, Charlie Hubbard, Peter Coleman, Tony Hooper, Charles Vickery; front: Les Richards, Roy Francis, Fred Jewell, Cecil Vickery (standing).

Ladies' Event on the Vicarage lawns, late 1800s.

Bellringers in the early 1900s outside the bell tower. Until the 1980s the Parochial Church Council took the ringers on an annual fishing trip to Beer and Lyme Regis.

*Celebrating 60 years of the WI in the old hut, 1977. Left to right, back row: Joan Partridge,
Jeane Walkley, Mrs Bates, Rose Lock, B. Bowles, Joyce Reeves, Audrey Johnson;
front: Mrs Collett, Mrs Seaman, Madge Stace, Mrs Woods, Gladys Turner, Ivy Hurst, Mrs Stone.*

WOMEN'S INSTITUTE IN CREECH

In 1917, a meeting was held in the schoolroom to see if there was any interest in forming a group. The meeting was well attended and Miss Slessor of Curvalion House was elected President, with Miss Sommerville of Ruishton as House Secretary and Mrs Hurrell (the schoolmaster's wife) as Treasurer. During the next three years the group established itself with meetings held regularly in the schoolroom at 2 shillings a time. These gatherings were always held on a Friday as the schoolroom screens could be removed (at 2s.6d. extra), and the caretaker could stoke the fire, put on lights and offer crockery for tea. The Institute heard that the Government was giving grants towards village halls, so they applied with the help of the Parish Council but were unlucky in their bid. Undaunted and determined, they decided to go ahead on their own to raise funds and get a hall. It was quite innovative at the time for women to look for land and building by themselves, but they were successful and Mr George Coombes agreed to give land close to the school. They heard of an ex-Army hut for sale at Cannington and bought it for £85.

In 1923 the new Village Hall was opened, and from this time onwards the members could hold meetings when they liked and could hire the building out to others. In 1924, records show that they were busy with local and national affairs. They purchased a pram for a new mother and gave tea to pensioners in the parish. In 1928 they were helping with clothes and aid for distressed miners in Durham and during the war they were blood donors and helped to raise money in many ways to help war victims. In 1953 they were at the forefront of aid efforts to help the flood victims at Lynmouth. Always respected for their interest and work for rural areas at local and government level, the WI in Creech St Michael survives, but alas without their building. This was condemned in 1993 and removed to make way for new houses, but the group meet in other places, keeping alive a country tradition lasting 83 years in the parish.

The hut just before demolition in 1994.

By direction of the Representatives of the late George Coombe. Esq.

Particulars

OF

The Charlton Estate

AT

Creech St. Michael and North Curry,

COMPRISING

CHARLTON HOUSE AND LANDS	101 Acres,
CHARLTON FARM	102 Acres,
COURT BARTON FARM	170 Acres,
SMALL HOLDING	25 Acres,

HAM WATER POWER MILLS,

COTTAGES, and Highly Valuable ACCOMMODATION LANDS,

comprising a total Area of

A. 401   2 r.   21 p.

WHICH

MESSRS.

C. R. MORRIS, SONS & PEARD

will offer for SALE BY AUCTION in Lots as herein set out (if not previously disposed of privately),

At the CASTLE HOTEL, TAUNTON,

On SATURDAY, 21st SEPTEMBER, 1929,

At 3 p.m. precisely.

These Particulars of Sale may be obtained at the Offices of the Auctioneers at North Curry and Taunton, where a Plan of the Lots may be seen; or from

Messrs. CHANNER & CHANNER,

Solicitors, Taunton, Milverton & Wiveliscombe.

Sale Poster for Charlton Estate, 1929.

Chapter 17
People and Places

CHARLTON

The name indicates that a settlement was a ceorlton, a place where a king's own husbandman lived and tilled the land, partly for himself and partly for the king. It is a common name throughout the country, and shows the original owner to have been favoured by the king, but managing an estate within a manor.

There are two old houses in Charlton, one Charlton House and the other Charlton Manor (originally called Charlton Farm, but renamed some years ago). Legend has it that a house stood on the site of Charlton Manor in King John's time, but the first recorded sale of the house was in 1558, when William Knapman (lord of the manor), sold a house, a dovecote and 138 acres of land to Alexander Sydenham.

Charlton Orchard

Charlton was only part of the estate sold, and Sydenham, who bought it and used it as an investment, bequeathed it to his daughter, Elizabeth, who married Sir John Poinzt of Gloucester. In turn she sold it to the first family to live in it and farm the land, who were the Pocockes. They appear to have been tenants before purchasing the farm, and continued to farm it for many years. The tomb of John Pococke lies within the Charlton Chapel in the church.

Edward Cely lived in the house, and in 1782 left it to his niece, who then sold to Richard Bullen who, after several years, began to extend it. Architecturally, the building is a puzzle, as it has been altered and added to many times, with old materials being used and some parts even falling down and never rebuilt. Investigation by an historical society in the early 1990s seemed to prove that there were originally two buildings, side by side at first, then joined. Certainly, the kitchen and dairy end of the house is older than the front, which seems to have been added when the owners became more prosperous in the 18th century.

The sitting room has an Adam fireplace, and the whole of the Georgian frontage was probably built about 1816, when large bills were recorded for work undertaken by Bullen, the owner

Since this time, the house has changed hands many times, being used to store farm equipment and hay, and at other times, as a restaurant. As a family home it has much charm, and the last few owners have enhanced its assets so that it remains a fine example of a country house (from notes supplied by Ansell Egerton).

CHARLTON ORCHARD

A farm with orchards has stood on this site for centuries, so apple trees would have filled the area around Charlton Farm. The house and farm were sold with the then owner building a new house in the fields and planting four acres of dessert fruit. Gradually, more land was bought and trees planted until the whole extended to its present size of approximately 16 hectares. Over 30 varieties of apples are grown here, as well as plums, pears, damsons, quince and soft fruit.

George Coombe of Charlton had his own smithy, which was in the grounds of Charlton Farm and consisted of two cottages and the forge itself. He owned land from Worthy Lane to Charlton, and was not very popular when he diverted several streams to feed his small mill and smithy. He invented a moveable sheep hurdle, which won a prize at the Royal Bath and West Show, but he was not a well-liked figure. He owned a Rolls Royce, but preferred to ride a horse or a three wheeled bicycle. The lane to Charlton was overhung with big trees, and he rode his charge at speed down through the lane, causing sparks to fly from the horse's shoes – people around about said that 'he rode like the devil'. In 1929, he died intestate, and all his land, including Charlton, Court Barton and Ham Mill went for auction.

Charlton House at Charlton. The date 1791 is scratched on a wall within the house.

Charlton folk, 1920.

THE STEVENS FAMILY

The Stevens family have resided in the parish of Creech since the 13th century, and were well known for 250 years for providing a service as blacksmiths. The first Stevens blacksmith was listed in 1749, and the last, William Stevens, was born in 1880. After he left school, he became apprenticed to his father and became the fifth generation of Creech blacksmiths.

Although he worked at the smithy, he wanted to be a soldier, and in 1899 he enlisted in the Royal Engineers and became number 2985. In 1890 he went to South Africa to take part in the Boer War, distinguishing himself by being awarded the Queen's South African Medal and the King's South African Medal.

Two years after his return to England, he was appointed as Shoeing and Carriage Smith, and was later made a Corporal. In 1913, he was promoted to a Farrier Sergeant, thereby making use of his previous apprenticeship at Creech. At the outbreak of the First World War he went to France, and in 1916 he was awarded the French Medaille Millitaire for distinguished service. This was followed by a Distinguished Conduct Medal 'for conspicuous coolness and devotion to duty in attending to wounded horses while the horses were being heavily shelled.'

On 22 March 1920 he was discharged from the Army with a pension for life, having become deaf and suffering bouts of malaria. His discharge sheet stated that he was a smart, sober and efficient farrier, and horses under his care were maintained to a high standard.

William Stevens then returned to Creech St Michael and took over from his father as the village blacksmith until 1939, when he retired and the business ceased. He lived a long life dying at the age of 90 in 1970. As he had no son, a great family of blacksmiths finally came to an end with his death.

Above: *William Stevens, Farrier Sergeant, 1916.*
Below: *William Stevens (centre) working in the forge, 1920.*

Leaving presentation to dinner ladies Mrs Stevens (centre) and Mrs Sandford (left), 1969.
Also present are teacher Miss Goddard (far left), head John Powell (fourth from left) and Revd Jones
(far right).

Presentation to Dr J. Caray and Mrs Carey on his retirement. Headmaster John Powell is to the left
of the picture and also present are school governors and children.

A painting of the Tone by Harry Frier.

HARRY FRIER

Born in 1849 in Edinburgh, Harry Frier was to have a connection with Creech St Michael as an artist who painted scenes in the area. His father, who was a manufacturer of stockings, decided late in life to become an artist, so from an early age Harry had a grounding in drawing. In 1860, his father gave up business for art and in 1867 Harry entered Edinburgh School of Art. In 1878 he moved to London and there, whilst scenery painting, met Kezia Catherine Dyer, the fourth child of George and Jemima Dyer of Creech St Michael. George died in 1872 and left property to Jemima at Bathpool and Thorney Biers on the canal at Creech where Kate and her younger sister Charlotte lived.

Kezia (Kate) and Harry married at Taunton Registry Office in 1881 and they lived in Bathpool. Harry rented a room in Taunton as a studio, and began to look for customers by frequenting the public houses in Taunton. He gradually built up a reputation as the commissions came in. But after 13 years of marriage disillusion set in. Kate had not produced a family and Harry was not making a living from painting. In 1899, Jemima died and was buried at Creech St Michael, and after this the relationship deteriorated, with Harry drinking and Kate struggling to make ends meet. Kate caught a chill which turned to bronchitis, and in February 1913 she died and was buried in Creech.

Harry was inconsolable, but with the help of his niece, Lotty, with whom he now lived, he managed to carry on, although he became very difficult and showed signs of senility. Lottie could not cope, and Harry went into the Poor Law Institute in Taunton. After six weeks he pleaded to return to Lottie's, and was in and out of the workhouse for several months.

In February 1921, he died there and was buried in Creech St Michael churchyard with his wife. The site of the grave is not known.

His prolific output of paintings of the area included several of Creech, and depict the canal and main street as well as river scenes. An exhibition of his work was shown in Taunton in 1998 and many of his pictures are now in the County Museum.

Thorney Biers or Thorneybees, the house on the canal where Harry Frier once lived.

Far left: *Dennis and Nora Drewe at Old Slaughter House, 1947 - this is now the site of Norden Bungalow.*

Left: *Parish Councillor Charles Harvey was a well-known figure in Creech. He lived at Brookings behind the chapel for many years and members of his family still live in the parish.*

Left: *The two Miss Orchards, well-loved village personalities. They lived in Hill Villa and their father was (in 1910) the Highway Surveyor for Taunton. The Miss Orchards now live in North Curry.*

Above: *Gladys Batstone who lived with her family at Laurel Villa, Northend. For many years she played the church organ and the piano at village 'sixpenny hops'. She was also Treasurer for the WI.*

Above: *William George Drewe at Northend, 1940.*

Left: *Mrs Hooper who, with her husband, was school caretaker for many years. She lived in Pig Barrel Lane, close to Curvalion House.*

Far left: *Doug Hooper, the butcher who took over Bishop's Shop.*

BOBBETTS

Throughout the parish records, the name Bobbett has appeared for over 354 years, beginning with a list (of militia) in 1569, until the last mention in the early 1900s of Miss Bobbett of Foxhole, being carried in her coffin along the canal bank. She seems to have been the last Bobbett to live in Creech.

The first Bobbett appears in the list of people who were eligible for the militia and the family also possessed arms which were listed. Thomas Bobbet was a light horseman, and as there were few horses recorded, he was probably regarded as essential to the cause.

From this time through the 16th and 17th centuries, the name is entered in many records. In 1665 Mary Bobbett had six fireplaces when the hearth tax was registered, which implied that she probably lived in a relatively modest house in the parish. Some of her family lived in Ham at this time and also registered hearths. In the churchwardens' accounts the following appears: 'Paid Edmund Bobbetts man for killing a polecat.' The name often crops up in places such as this.

The family seem to have lived in the mill in Ham, in Northend, in Coal Harbour and Foxhole. In the 1730s, a survey of the parish gave Richard and John Bobbett 45 acres of land, yet in 1789 a Timothy Bobbett appears on the poor book list as requiring clothes. Every position in the parish from constable to lawbreaker was filled by a member of the Bobbett family. In 21 years of baptisms, from 1668 to 1689 in the parish, eight sons and eight daughters were born to Bobbetts, so it is not surprising that they feature so regularly.

When the Act to make the River Tone navigable to Taunton was proposed, the principle objectors were Richard and Robert Bobbett, who worked Ham Mill and owned trows which carried coal from Wales and also grain, wool and cloth to Bridgwater, and thence up the river to the mill and then by smaller boat or pony to Taunton. If the Act was passed, the Bobbetts could see their lucrative business disappearing, so they objected most strongly. But in 1699, when the Act was eventually passed, traders found the tolls too high and many still unloaded at Ham Wharves and had their goods transported by pack pony. Thus the Bobbetts remained in business.

By 1740, John Bobbett and his daughter Joan owned a cottage and garden known as The Ship Inn in Bull Street, directly in front of The Riverside. The buildings were removed in the 1960s, but it seemed a strange place to have two public houses so close. Perhaps The Ship Inn was there as a pub before the Church House became a public house. Records do not tell us whether or not the Bobbetts were publicans, so perhaps they just owned the property.

William Bobbett farmed at Cathill by the canal in 1894, and was one of the first parish councillors, so the last Miss Bobbett was probably his daughter or sister. As a last comment on this populous family, I received a phone call in 1994 from a Mrs Bobbett, whose husband had traced his family back to King Alfred, but he had sadly died before I could look at his findings. No doubt Bobbetts still live around the area and would be interested in how their family had helped to shape our parish for so many years.

Cathill, once the home of the Bobbetts. The last of the family died in the early 1900s and Jack Sweeting farmed here for many years.

Early-20th century photograph of a group of villagers – cleverly the photographer managed to include himself in the shot!

View from the church tower, 1910.

A WALK AROUND THE VILLAGE

The Vicarage stood opposite the entrance to Hyde Lane until recent times. The old house was one of several vicarages in Creech. One was removed when the canal was built and was by Vicarage Farm. The red brick building in Vicarage Lane is now two dwellings, and the author remembers it as a big draughty old place which the incumbent found diffi- cult to heat, but where several village whist drives were held, as well as other meetings. The old Vicarage mentioned at Hyde Lane had an Air Raid Warden's post in the shed in the garden during the Second World War, and at the time of writing the area is being redeveloped for housing.

Arundells, the estate agents, is a very old property, and where the first few houses are in Hyde Lane there was a huge barn, a part of the wall still remains. The whole area was Arundells Farm and at one time was owned by the Foxwell family. Benjamin Foxwell was the landlord of the Bell Inn for several years.

At the entrance to West View at Northend, there was a riding stable run by Mrs Alexander for many years. A part of the wall still stands by the first bungalow. Horses were very much part of the scene in the village until the redevelopment.

Dillons was also a farm, and the owner had a lifelong house keeper who always walked a little behind him when he went to church on Sundays. The whole house was surrounded by dark fir trees and had an air of mystery. The farm was sold and Dillons Road came into being. At Northend, the road went past the undertakers toward what was Northend Mill to Langaller, and the original way can still be traced across the main road and by the motorway. Manor Farm was well off the road until the new way was made.

Behind the chapel there was a row of council houses called Ryes Terrace, which were discovered to have little foundations in recent years and were pulled down to make way for more development.

In the Holly Cottage near the chapel lived the baker, Billy Brass, who was a well-known figure in the village, for as well as being the baker he was a photographer and owned some of the early cameras with which he took many pictures of the village – some survive and are a wonderful record of a Somerset village. He used to display them in the roadside window of Holly Cottage and changed the display regularly. The author remembers his willing- ness to share his photographs, especially when his sight was going. Alas, the pictures are no longer available for public view.

At Charlton Road there was a shop facing up the road and for many years it remained closed and decaying. Joe Way and his sister ran the general store, but had a feud with the Morrell family, who ran a road-haulage company in the area. Tradition has it that when a member of the Morrell family entered the shop one day, Joe Way, closed it and never opened it again. He owned a monkey which once damaged the thatch on the Morrell's house. The Crown Inn, a little way up the lane from Joe Way, was nicknamed The Drum and Monkey, as one of the pub customers played the drum in the village band and Joe Way took the monkey there.

For many years, the village Flower Show and Gymkhana was held on the aqueduct field at Cheats Corner. Horse-riders came from miles around to compete in the first round of the Foxhunter Competition. The Gymkhana was run by Tacker Sweeting and helpers, his love of horses making him an ideal person to do this. In recent years he worked very hard to continue the tradition of the Gymkhana by holding an event for charity where youngsters, rid- ing horses from his own stables as well as their own, took part. After many years as a familiar figure riding his horses through Creech and serving 46 years on the Parish Council, Tacker Sweeting died early in 2000.

Standing in an important position in the main street, Arundells was probably built in the 1600s and was once thatched. This was replaced in 1929 with tiles, and there have been considerable alterations to the interior over the years. Opposite Arundells there were two thatched cottages. In one lived the village boot and shoemaker, Oliver Haskins and his wife. In 1957, the cottages caught fire and were demolished. The garage and Post Office now stand on the site, but some of the old photographs show the cottages with their thatched roofs.

Some Somerset words used within living memory include: twink (chaffinch), yel (eel), nill (nail), fret (basket), gaern (garden), gammet (fun sport), mommick (scarecrow), larmy (sorrowful), dimpsy (getting dark), pickle (hay fork), haddel (heap), snicky (small field), skitty (moorhen), gaffle (dung fork), keep (large basket), maid (any young female) and to once (sudden happening).

In 1910, Dillons House was sold with 10 acres – 'a valuable orchard fully stocked with choicest varieties of table apples and plums'. The trees were 'well grown and in full bearing'.

This shop at the end of Northend was a butcher's for many years...

...then it was a bakery. Now it is a funeral director's.

Arundells.

Old Vicarage opposite Hyde Lane, now demolished and the site of a small estate.

Curvallion House, probably built in 1815 – Savidge the brick-maker lived there. It has had many tenants. In the 1960s it was made into flats, but has since reverted back to a single house.

Laburnum Terrace was built to house mill workers. The last house at the road end was once a butchers, and in one of the gardens at the back, an entrepreneur made ginger beer.

ON 1 SEPTEMBER 2000, AS MANY BUSINESSES IN THE PARISH AS POSSIBLE WERE RECORDED AND PHOTOGRAPHED. THESE ARE NOW SET DOWN AS PART OF THE HISTORY OF CREECH AND SHOW THE EVER-CHANGING FACE OF WORK AND EMPLOYMENT IN THE COMMUNITY.

Above: *The pedigree herd of Simmental bulls in Charlton Lane belongs to Nigel Jamieson who runs Charlton Fruit and Flower Farm. Strawberries, flowers, foliage and beans are grown in season. The holding has been there since 1984.*

Top left: *Sedgemoor Honey Farm is run by Chris Harries from his home in West View. He has been in business for 20 years and has 200 hives over a large area of the county, including Exmoor where he gathers heather honey, a speciality of his. The hives are hired out to orchards such as Charlton who have about 25 in the blossom time. Chris travels many miles to service his hives and collect the honey which he sells to local shops.*

Second from top: *Bigwood Partners have an agricultural engineers company in a prominent position at Walford Cross. Local farmers find the business very useful, especially at times of crisis when vital machinery breaks down. The company also sells tractors and other machinery. It stands on the site of an old garage and tea shop owned by Stanley Best. Keith Bigwood lives in Creech and is a strong supporter of village activities.*

Third from top: *The blacksmith, Martin Wright, has a thriving metalwork business following the pattern of generations of blacksmiths at the same forge. Will Stevens was one of the village smiths who worked there (until 1939). Martin repairs and services garden equipment as well as specialising in ironwork and welding. He has been in business in Creech for eight years.*

Bottom: *Drakes Farm at Creech Heathfield specialises in growing and packing potatoes. H. Bult and Sons have recently built new stores at the farm and sell locally in the Taunton and Bridgwater area.*

Above: *Alpine Cattery and pet food suppliers is situated on the road to Ham and has been in business for nine years. They sell a range of animal feedstuffs and also board cats whilst their owners are away. Mr and Mrs Jenkins are local to the area, one of Mr Jenkins' relations having once been the village constable.*

Top left: *Farm diversification has changed the calf-rearing unit of J. Sweeting at Vicarage Farm to S.P. Motors dealing in quality used vehicles.*

Left: *Vale Labels is a small business offering printing services for large and small companies alike. At the time of writing it is situated at Brickyard Farm at the end of Bull Street but is due to move to a premises at the paper mill at the end of September 2000. The company has been in existence for nine years and is a family partnership. Mike Riches is looking to expand in more convenient premises with easier access in future.*

Left: *Langdons Industries, on a ten-acre site close to the M5 and on the edge of the parish, was established in 1980 on the old Tate and Lyle site at Walford Cross. It is a distribution centre with an emphasis on chilled foods for the grocery trade. Its 100 vehicles and 120 trailers regularly deliver to grocery outlets across a wide area of the country and the 18 000 pallets in chill storage ensure correct management of frozen and chilled foods. The Managing Director is M. Holder and the company employs local people in all sections.*

Left: *This is the car sales service of Corbett and Hall. David Corbett is the present owner and has been in Creech for some 20 years. Alongside this is J.V. Garages owned by J. Vallance where cars are serviced and repaired. The present owner is due to go into partnership under the name B.L.F. Motors. A garage of some kind has been on this site for over 40 years.*

Above: *David Boggan has been established as an estate agent in Creech since 1985. He has expanded the business to include lettings and deals with a wide range of properties both locally and in Taunton. David lives on the premises in one of the oldest village properties. His wife Jenny is a designer florist and makes bouquets and arrangements for all occasions.*

Top left: *Roger Fell is the Postmaster and has run the Post Office at its present site for six years. A vital service for the parish, there has been a Post Office in Creech since 1830.*

Second from top: *The Londis has been run by Mrs S. Phillips for over a year. The shop has a wide range of products in stock and, situated in the village centre on a site where a shop has existed for generations, it is a useful service for many without transport.*

Third from top: *In 1890 two Creech families were joined in marriage when William Hopkins, butcher, married Emma Howe, daughter of the village grocer. These are the grandparents of the present owner of Hopkins which has operated since 1890 at its present premises and throughout the two World Wars. From 1940 to 1954, the company was under Government control in the guise of the Ministry of Food when nearly all output was dispatched by GWR to London. A.C. Hopkins has maintained business relations with Smithfield Market since the 1920s although the market is only a fraction of its former size.*

Bottom: *Established in 1985, Somerset Caravans and Camping Equipment is one of the oldest retail caravan companies in the county. Alongside the sale of caravans, they have a well-equipped accessory centre selling everything for camping and caravanning. Tim Harlow, the Managing Director, has hopes for the company to expand in the near future.*

Above: *Taunton Vale Golf Club was opened in 1991 taking land owned by Ron Welch and Mead Loxton, both local farmers. It covers 156 acres but has two courses, the Cherton 18-hole and the Durston 9-hole. The club is a popular venue and its courses challenging with hidden greens and watercourses. Also on the complex is a restaurant, equipment shop, club house and luxury changing rooms. The greens offer wide-ranging views over the Vale of Taunton.*

Top left: *Creech Fruit and Vegetable Shop provides fresh, often local, produce to customers from around the parish. Derek Hancock the owner has premises at the paper mill for storage and he provides a delivery service to local shops. Zella Hector and Angela Barry are seen here arranging the outdoor display which attracts customers to the shop.*

Second from top: *Creech Heathfield Salon is run by Sarah Hunt who in 1997 renovated a small hairdressing business into a thriving beauty salon offering a wide range of services. Sarah has customers from a wide area and is pictured here outside the shop which has seen many changes in its 40 years of business.*

Third from top: *Adjoining the Post Office is another hairdressers run by Caroline Oates who has had the business for four years. Her friendly salon offers a convenient service for local people.*

Bottom: *Creech St Michael Funeral Directors was established five years ago by Nigel Ford at the premises that had previously been a butchers, then a bakery-cum-butchers since 1960. Nigel and his staff provide an essential service to the locality. Nigel is pictured outside the premises at Northend with Melanie Ball.*

Another business, not pictured here, is that of John Hunt, who runs a transport company at Northend delivering animals all over the country. The family, farmers and nurserymen from early times, have been in the village since the 1300s.

Above: *Within the paper mill there are a number of small units housing businesses ranging from tyre sales to County Hardwoods. Taunton Deane own the units and they are ideal for small companies just starting out. The units are constantly changing but are a useful asset for the parish providing employment for several people. It is good to see the long-established mill premises put to use again.*

Second from top: *One of the companies based at the premises, Mill Auto Services.*

Left: *Charlton Orchards has been growing fruit for over 50 years. Cider trees grew on the same site centuries ago. The orchards use local labour at harvest time and supply local shops with fruit in season. Over the years the range of products has extended to apple juice, preserves, herbs and unusual vegetables. The business is a partnership between Matthew Freudenberg and Robin Small and is well known for the wide range of apple varieties available.*

Bottom: *Where once there was a tree and shrub nursery a new company now sells garden fertiliser and wood mulch at Creech Heathfield opposite Castle Villa.*

IN ADDITION TO THE BUSINESSES RECORDED HERE THERE ARE ARE A GREAT NUMBER OF HOME-BASED VENTURES SERVING THE COMMUNITY. ALL OF THE PEOPLE OFFERING A SERVICE ARE FOLLOWING A TRADITION OF LOCAL INDUSTRY AND ENTERPRISE WHICH HAS EXISTED IN CREECH ST MICHAEL FOR HUNDREDS OF YEARS.

The village band gathered outside the church on the Coronation day of George V, 1911.

Conclusion

Creech St Michael, like many other parishes, had its history shaped by its inhabitants and their way of life. They worked hard, often for little reward, but they shared a sense of community and cared about their neighbours. They looked to alleviate poverty and handicap, deal wth crime and ensure that justice was done. Life was not all work and as the seasons changed so they celebrated harvest home, Whitsun, and the first days of cider making. As in all communities, gossip abounded and as seen at one session of the Vestry an eavesdropper was noted. What did he want to know? Four decades ago I was a young teacher with Mr S.C.K. Kingdon and as we stood in the school playground above the village street he told me tales of village people and events I have always remembered. Village gossip abounded then and my memories of those days probably fostered my interest in the inhabitants of the parish as the stories told were of families, celebrations, quarrels and kind deeds that happen in any community.

Life was about work, keeping the family together, and about knowing your neighbour and giving a helping hand when needed. All through the research for this volume these facts shone through and the need to record the way in which a parish cared for its people and its surroundings became important.

This parish is my parish. My children were born here, and we have lived and worked here for 43 years. I am indeed part of its history. Newcomers have become part of the parish, many widely travelled unlike those of years ago, who often never left the village or only journeyed short distances. Some 43 years ago when we arrived and visited The Bell Inn for the first time a local asked us where we came from. On being told High Wycombe he asked if it was near Weston-Super-Mare because he'd never been to Weston. Things have changed greatly since then and the speed of change is increasing. I hope that the parish does not alter too quickly and that we have time to to reflect on life over the centuries as depicted in this history.

I hope also that all who read this book will feel the sense of community which comes through the telling and celebrate the fact that the parish stands as it does today because of all those parishioners who have left their mark in some way on our lives.

On election day there would be some kind of brawling, but when this picture was taken it was peaceful. Creech had the nickname 'Quarrelsome Creech', and at election time it evidently lived up to its reputation.

Subscribers

David M. Arrowsmith, Ruishton, Somerset

Mrs L. J. and Miss J. A. Babb, Creech St Michael,
  Somerset

Betty Bail, Shepton Beauchamp, Somerset

Nan and Derek Baker, Creech Heathfield, Somerset

Mrs Margaret Bartlett, Creech St Michael, Somerset

Eleanor Ann Bastable (née Dunn), North Petherton,
  Somerset

Frederick W. Batstone, Creech St Michael, Somerset

Angela Susan Berry, Creech St Michael, Somerset

Mrs S. J. Betty, Bramley Road, Taunton, Somerset

George and Liz Blinko, Chard, Somerset

Anne Boase (née Greenshields), Edinburgh

David W. M. Boggon, Arundells House,
  Creech St Michael, Somerset

Mr and Mrs Boneham, Creech St Michael, Somerset

William and Patricia Booker, Ham, Somerset

M. J. Bowey, Creech St Michael, Somerset

John and Wendy Bowthorpe, Creech St Michael,
  Somerset

Mrs Jessie Brass, Creech Heathfield, Somerset

David Brown, Wellington, Somerset

Merlyn Brown, Creech St Michael, Somerset

Mrs Gwyneth M. Bryant, Creech St Michael, Somerset

C. C. Butters, Heathfield House, Creech Heathfield,
  Somerset

Mrs Doris Cann (née Mawdsley), Sheffield

Thomas Carter, Creech St Michael, Somerset

Sally and Reg Causley, Creech St Michael, Somerset

Roger and Suzanne Cavill, Creech Heathfield,
  Somerset

Deborah Chesshire, Creech St Michael, Somerset

Jean and Richard Child, Creech St Michael, Somerset

Mrs M. Chiswell, Creech St Michael, Somerset

Eric and Iris Chown, Creech St Michael, Somerset

Mr and Mrs A.M. Coakes, Creech Heathfield, Somerset

Joy Mary Coate (née Dunn), North Curry, Somerset

Elsie Coe

Sheldon Cole, formerly of Creech St Michael, Somerset

Ruth and Jim Cole, Creech St Michael, Somerset

Peter Cole, Creech St Michael, Somerset

Andrea Cornelius, Probus, Cornwall

Mr and Mrs Brian Cornelius, Hinton St George,
  Somerset

Mr and Mrs A. M. Covey, Langaller, Taunton, Somerset

L. A. Cowen, Creech St Michael, Somerset

Creech St Michael C. of E. Primary School,

Kelvin F. Davies, Creech St Michael, Somerset

Mrs Jane Davies (née Allen), Stisted, Essex

K. and L. Deeley, Creech St Michael, Somerset

Stella and Barrie Dixon, Creech Heathfield, Somerset

Tom and Iris Dominey, Creech St Michael, Somerset

Jessica Downer, Taunton, Somerset

Jonathan Downer, Maidstone, Kent

Juliette Downer, Barcelona, Spain

Sue and Clive Downer, Creech Heathfield, Somerset

Michael Drewe, Ontario, Canada

Gladys Nora Drewe, 'Norden', Creech St Michael,
  Somerset

Norman and Marion Drewe, Creech St Michael,
  Somerset

Graham Dunn, Creech St Michael, Somerset

Eric F. Dunn, Oake, Somerset

Phyllis M. Dye, Creech St Michael, Somerset

The Edis Family, Creech St Michael, Somerset

Wendy Egerton, Cape Peninsula, South Africa

Peter Elston, Thurloxton, Somerset

Mr and Mrs M. R. Evans, Creech St Michael, Somerset

Edward A. Ewens, Applehayes, Creech St Michael,
  Somerset

P. M. Exelby (née Hutchings), Creech St Michael,
  Somerset

Mr and Mrs B. W. Fairburn, Creech St Michael,
  Somerset

Mrs R. M. Farrow, Creech St Michael, Somerset

Nigel, Annette and Mark Finch, Langaller, Somerset

Derek and Denise Garrett, Creech St Michael,
  Somerset

Don Gates, Creech St Michael, Somerset

Madeline Geen, Creech St Michael, Somerset

Margaret Gibbins, Charlton Road, Creech Heathfield,
  Somerset

Martyn and Elaine Gossage, Creech St Michael,
  Somerset

Brenda Greed, Creech St Michael, Somerset

Oliver Harries, Creech St Michael, Somerset

Ruth Harries, Creech St Michael, Somerset

Mrs Jenny Harrington (née Allen), Chester, New Jersey

Rose E. Harris, Creech St Michael, Somerset

Mr Simon Harris, Creech Heathfield, Somerset

Malcolm and Monica Harvey, Creech Heathfield, Somerset
Maureen M. Haseman, Llanfoist, Gwent
Angela Heayns, Creech St Michael, Somerset (1960s)
Louise Hector, Creech St Michael, Somerset
Zella and Gerald Hector, Creech St Michael, Somerset
Donald and Evelyn Henshaw, Creech Heathfield, Somerset
B. J. and J. Hill, Creech St Michael, Somerset
Tony and Jan Hiscock, Creech St Michael, Somerset
Mr and Mrs I. Hitchen, Creech St Michael, Somerset
David and Lorraine Hooper, Creech St Michael, Somerset
G. Hooper, Creech St Michael, Somerset
Mr and Mrs V. J. House, Creech Heathfield, Somerset
Matt and Vanessa Howe, Creech Heathfield, Somerset
Ken Hunt, Creech Heathfield, Somerset
Frederick D. Hunt, Creech St Michael, Somerset
Shirley A. Hunt, Creech St Michael, Somerset
John W. Hunt, Creech St Michael, Somerset
Christine Hurford, Creech St Michael, Somerset
Ethel M. Jenkins, Creech St Michael, Somerset
Mr and Mrs A. E. Jenkins, North End, Creech St Michael, Somerset
Gwen and Frank Jones, Creech St Michael, Somerset
Revd Ken and Sheila Jones, Taunton, Somerset
David and Valerie Laing, Creech St Michael, Somerset
Philip and Ann Laing, California
Famille Leclercq, Fierville Les Parcs, France
Carol Leese, Creech St Michael, Somerset
Mr and Mrs J. Liddall, North End, Creech St Michael
Mrs B. Lock, Creech Heathfield, Somerset
Mr W. H. Lock, Torquay, Devon
Mr Austen Lock, Creech St Michael, Somerset
Mrs E. Manning, Ham
Mildred R. Manuel, Creech Heathfield, Somerset
Mrs V. M. Marlborough, Creech St Michael, Somerset
Matthew Martin, Cleeve, North Somerset
Ben Martin, Cleeve, North Somerset
Alison J. Martin, Cleeve, North Somerset
Sammy Martin, Cleeve, North Somerset
Daphne Matthews, formerly Greenshields
Kim L. Mauri, Croydon, Surrey
Lesley McDowall, Creech St Michael, Somerset
Janet and Douglas McKay, Creech St Michael, Somerset
Kirstin McKay, Monkton Heathfield, Somerset
Revd Lewis Misselbrook, Creech St Michael, Somerset
Merce Moret, Creech St Michael, Somerset
Tony and Jenny Murray, Ham, Somerset
Paul, Heather, Christopher and Michael Nation, Creech St Michael, Somerset
Martin Nation, Creech St Michael, Somerset
Alan G. Norton, Creech St Michael, Somerset
Danny O'Sullivan F.Inst. D., Creech St Michael, Somerset
The Old Police Station

Mike and Cilla Owen, Coalharbour House, Ham, Somerset
Mrs Gertrude M. Pearn (née Hunt), Weston-super-Mare, Somerset
Michael J. Pendry, Monkton Heathfield, Taunton, Somerset
John and Josephine Pentney, Creech St Michael, Somerset
Cliff Perrin, ex Creech St Michael, Somerset
Philip Perryman, Creech St Michael, Somerset
Helen Phillips, Willowbank, Creech St Michael, Somerset
Janet A. Pike, Creech Heathfield, Somerset
Mrs P. Powell, Creech St Michael, Somerset
County Councillor Hazel Prior-Sankey,
A. Pugh-Thomas, West Monkton, Somerset
Sue Rhys-Davies, Creech Heathfield, Somerset
Sue Richards, Taunton, Somerset
P. A. Richards, Creech St Michael, Somerset
Leslie T. Richards J.P., Creech St Michael, Somerset
Donald F. Salt, Creech St Michael, Somerset
Tina G. Sikes, Creech St Michael, Somerset
Pirjo and Sampo Siskonen, Mikkeli St Michael, Finland
Chris, Lesley, Jessica and James Small, High Wycombe, Bucks.
Anthony C. Small
Len and Barbara Squire, Creech St Michael, Somerset
Madge Stace, Creech St Michael, Somerset
Nick Stone, Creech Heathfield, Somerset
Katrina Sulley (née McKay), Basingstoke, Hants.
Jean and Tom Summerfield, Creech St Michael, Somerset
John S. Sweeting, Creech St Michael, Somerset
Michael C. Thomas, Llangaller
Michael Tolchard, Creech St Michael, Somerset
Mrs Lesley Toms, Creech St Michael, Somerset
Heather Tout, Ashill, Somerset
Sally Tuer, Creech Heathfield, Taunton, Somerset
Frederick J. Vile, Creech St Michael, Somerset
Jeanne H. Walker, Creech St Michael, Somerset
John F. W. Walling, Newton Abbot, Devon
Jean Walters and Family, Creech St Michael, Somerset
Lisa and Ian Warren, Creech St Michael, Somerset
Eileen Webb, Creech Heathfield, Somerset
Mr Adrian J. Webb, Taunton, Somerset
Mrs Margaret F. Webb (née Pearn), Weston-super-Mare, Somerset
Peggy F. Webber, Creech St Michael, Somerset
Sue Whitehead, Salisbury
M. T. and B. I. Wildman, Creech St Michael, Somerset
Kay Wilson, Creech St Michael, Somerset
Joan Wright, Creech St Michael, Somerset
Jean and Alan Wright, Cirencester, Glos.
Dr and Mrs J. D. Wrout, Ham, Creech St Michael, Somerset
Jane E. Wyatt, Creech Heathfield, Somerset

ALSO AVAILABLE IN THE SERIES

SOME OF THE MANY TITLES AVAILABLE IN 2001

For details of any of the above titles or if you are interested in writing your own community history, please contact: Community Histories Editor, Halsgrove House, Lower Moor Way, Tiverton Business Park, Tiverton, Devon EX16 6SS, England, e-mail:sales@halsgrove.com If you are particularly interested in any of the images in this volume, it may be possible to supply a copy. Please telephone 01884 243242 for details.